Planning Crime Prevention

Planning Crime Prevention

William Clifford
Australian Institute
of Criminology

Lexington Books
D.C. Heath and Company
Lexington, Massachusetts
Toronto

Library of Congress Cataloging in Publication Data

Clifford, William, 1918-
  Planning crime prevention.

  Includes index.
  1. Crime prevention—Planning. I. Title
HV7431.C58   364.4   75-42910
ISBN 0-669-00560-6

Published simultaneously in Canada.

Printed in the United States of America.

International Standard Book Number: 0-669-00560-6

Library of Congress Catalog Card Number: 75-42910

Contents

List of Figure and Table

Preface

This book is intended for those who have to learn or teach crime prevention planning as well as the general reader; it is based on a paper prepared for the First United Nations Interregional Course on Social Defence Planning, which was held in Sydney, Australia in November of 1975. It also incorporates the lectures which I delivered at the First Course on Social Defence Planning held at the United Nations Asia and Far East Institute for the Prevention of Crime and the Treatment of Offenders, Fuchu, Tokyo, Japan in February and March cf 1972. However, the lectures have been redrafted as necessary to encompass later developments and to provide what is intended to be initial training in crime prevention planning.

Social defence and *crime prevention* are equated in the chapters that follow, the term *crime prevention* being preferred to avoid the problems of definition and emphasis that have dogged the progress of social defence as a policy concept. Crime prevention, anyway, is far more than social and is narrowly, if not mistakenly, perceived as defence. Crime prevention planning is also far wider in scope than the idea of criminal justice planning, which has been used in some countries to refer to planning within the criminal justice system, i.e., police, courts, and corrections. Crime prevention planning incorporates this but reaches out to any and many other sectors of the economy that have significance for crime.

This explanation will also indicate that the term *crime prevention* is used in its widest literal sense and therefore is more extensive and intensive than the areas encompassed by the crime prevention units, which a number of Western police forces have set up to deal with security precautions, to prevent crime or to encourage more effective community cooperation with the police. In this book crime prevention is conceived of as a concern of the total economic and social organization and as a part of the general development of society.

Chapter 1 is intended for readers with no previous acquaintance with the subject of planning and only a general idea of what is meant by planning for crime prevention. Chapter 2 traces the meaning and practice of national planning with its economic and social planning components. This is the context of crime prevention and ends with a discussion of the interrelationships between crime prevention and other general sectors of the economy. Chapter 3 then deals with more specific issues in crime prevention planning and ends with some national crime prevention planning experiences.

Inevitably the arguments overlap between the chapters, and there is a certain amount of unavoidable repetition. But since the collection of chapters is intended to constitute a course, this may have advantages in both teaching and learning.

1 Preliminary Considerations

Planning in Wonderland

While much of the behavioral transformation of modern societies can be viewed dispassionately as the inevitable consequence of economic development and social change (as a necessary part of the transition of a society from one stage of growth to another), it is becoming increasingly evident that many of the negative and detrimental consequences of change flow from the conspicuous inability of societies to prepare and provide for them.

Not only has there been a pursuit of long-term benefits without counting the short-term costs[a] (or a desire for immediate returns without calculating the delayed reactions[b]), but hindsight now reveals an incapacity of most societies to provide adequately for such noxious phenomena as pollution and crime, even when it is quite possible to forecast it. This means that there has been a hidden hopefulness about planning in the past—an unreality—a planning, in effect, for a wonderland that we can never achieve.

The twentieth session of the United Nations' Commission for Social Development (January 1969) considered, under item seven of its agenda, the social aspects of the preparations then being made for the Second United Nations Development Decade. On the subject of general principles for the formulation of its goals and policies it observed:

> Social goals and programs will also have to be formulated relating to the major undesirable social phenomena which accompany economic development, industrialization, and rapid urbanization. These ... may relate to such problems as slums and shanty towns, air and water pollution, disease, crime and delinquency, problems of child care and youth preparation, the weakening of mutual assistance accompanying the breaking up of the traditional family or tribe, and so on.

It is grievously apparent that, as regards crime, practically no heed has been paid to this advice. While in the preparation of national development plans there has been more attention given to the quality of life, the reduction or minimizing

[a]One example would be long range national development plans for newly independent countries with no remedies for immediate problems of unemployment likely to have political consequences.

[b]For example, the denuding of forests or the discharging of polluted chemical waste into rivers and lakes, or the rushing of funds into projects without sufficient thought given to the possible reactions to their mismanagement.

1

of pollution, and the control of housing and disease, this concern has not yet brought crime prevention into the heart of national planning. Though dramatic and newsworthy crimes dominate the media, force people to move out of high-risk neighborhoods, and sustain a vast new industry of security guards, locking and safety devices, watch dogs, and alarms, still we plan as if humans were never irrational, frustrated, unhappy, or perverse. We plan still for the needs of the law abiding, ignoring their fears of housebreak, robbery, and personal violence and disregarding the exploitation of the law abiding by those who are not. This is a little bit like building a house without the indelicacy of a toilet, or like scientists considering only the use of their research and not its abuse.

Despite its notorious effect on the quality of life, crime has been accorded relatively little planning attention. Few measures are contemplated to provide for the detrimental effects of an unremitting corrosion of the cohesive informal social controls as older or traditional patterns of living have been deranged by the pace of urban, commercial, and/or industrial growth. And in the past there has been something not quite respectable about trying to divert the planner's gaze from his blueprints, economic and social indicators, and the shape of a new and perhaps model society to the vandalism and venality that were boring holes in the woodwork of the plan before it was half erected.

The glaring deficiencies in planning for future crime prevention and control have not all been due to administrative myopia, the hollowness of economic models, or to the unthinking neglect of the behavioral or social changes initiated or accelerated by investments in national development. They have derived to a great extent from a conspicuous lack of crime prevention knowledge and, more particularly, from the dearth of technical information necessary for crime prevention planning. Being aware of likely crime trends has not always been the same as knowing what to do about them. There is still a woeful lack of material being published or communicated on how precisely to plan for less crime.

The techniques and skills necessary for crime prevention planning were unlikely, anyway, to flow from planners with eyes on hopeful but distant futures or still hypnotized by the redemptive mirage of an augmented GNP. For such credulous guides, higher incomes were always a panacea for social disequilibrium. The new conceptual tools for planning might have come from the sciences of social or individual development, but these have proved to be too broad, too narrow, or too dangerous to produce the models or devices required. They were too broad when they dealt with the issues of social change without reducing these to methods or practical recommendations related to our own times; they were too narrow when they concerned themselves with individuals or groups without reference to the decisions already being made for such units by planning authorities; and while neurosurgery, psychosurgery, biochemistry, and pharmocology offered clues to behavior modification via lobectomy, drugs, or medication, these had frightening dimensions and are increasingly excluded as a result of a widening concern for human dignity and human rights.

The earlier and overconfident bases for development thinking have been severely shaken by the food and energy shortages, unemployment, rising prices, and the worldwide experiences of a new kind of "stagflation." While all these have shown again mankind's capacity for unpredictable and irrational behavior, the persistence of greed and selfishness, the irrepressible nature of man's independence, and his supreme disregard for the many attempts to "type" human conduct, there have been no brilliant substitutions for the older economic models, based on closed systems with rational investment and consumption combining to provide income and employment with improvements in the quality of life. Such attempts as there have been to provide for ways of dealing with the new inflation-unemployment connection typically ignore the quite illegal activites that may have given rise to situations conducive to crisis. People still plan as if crime did not exist or as if human nature was perfect and predictable. Only very recently has attention been given to the importance of administrative dishonesty or bureaucratic deviance, to multinational circumvention of laws, and to the national and global significance of economic crime; but this has been unfamiliar territory for the economic and social planner and the criminologist alike.

The so-called short-term social, human, and political issues that were expected to yield to longer-term planning for a more prosperous society have proved resistant and recalcitrant; they have shown a new, vigorous, and hitherto unsuspected capacity to frustrate, distort, or even negate completely the longer-term plans. This has reached a point at which the quality of life and the claims of fairness and justice now actively compete for priority (or equal consideration at least) with the older and usual demands for higher and improved material benefits. Younger people especially have challenged the validity of previously unquestioned "benefits" of certain life styles.

At the same time, a social revolution in values has cast increasing doubt on the desirability of the older norms and has thereby affected the objects and targets of social engineering. The older precepts no longer apply. Formerly unquestioned "laws" now require reformulation and redrafting in new perspectives and proportions. There is, furthermore, the increasing evidence that via the extension of economic crime, the exploitation of consumers, the effects of internal corruption, and the spread of organized corporate crime no less than by the increasing recourse to violence, a stage may well have been reached at which new dimensions of crime are not only reflections of a disturbed society but are actually molding lifestyles and developing new social contours. Crime, which has always been the shadow of civilization, has in some countries become, or is threatening to become, the real substance—a driving force—of political as well as economic and social change.[c]

---

[c]This, incidentally, was a role assigned to crime in society by Aristotle. He saw crime as one of the agents of change; it got out of official control, forced readjustments in society, and thus promoted a change in the cycle.

Criminology itself has been more preoccupied with analyzing the past than delving into the future. Developmental criminology has not yet arrived. Some earlier criminological excursions into prediction techniques offered little of real value for the policy-makers at the macrolevel and could not always distinguish reliably between offenders and nonoffenders except by the questionable criteria of legal process. The accumulating evidence of a close (though not necessarily causal) relationship between development and crime has carried with it only peripheral information on the steps most likely to prevent and control crime. Further, the vast amounts spent on increasing opportunities for the poor and the strengthening of law and order in some countries has been so accompanied by rising rates of more serious and more violent crime that existing services and current concepts of crime prevention have been opened to vigorous challenge.

The attempt to plot crime rates as functions of economic well-being or depression has a long but rather undistinguished history, which makes it all the more surprising that some people are inclined to rewrite criminology as political science and interpret *all* crime as due to injustice and underprivilege. It appears on the evidence available that we can get as much (if not more) crime from affluence as from depression, and, on a world view, we can get as much negative deviation from the established norms where there is a surfeit as where there is a deficiency of resources.[d] Inequalities do not necessarily account for the differences between countries with more and countries with less crime. There are notoriously hierarchical and discriminatory societies that have little crime.

The more recent shift in criminological thinking from the examination of offenders to the scrutiny of the kind of criminal justice systems, which separate and label some but not others, which discriminate sometimes unjustly, and which often manifest an internal inconsistency in procedures and values, has been timely but not particularly productive of either wise or specific counsel for those charged with the investment of public funds. Much could be said about what not to do, but little of a positive or directive nature.

Finally, the most radical recasting of crime as a function of the distribution of power in certain ideologies and of criminology as an aegis for action, confrontation, and reform leaves conflict and open revolution as questionable solutions for a problem that has always beset, and is still plaguing, countries of vastly different political persuasions. Rather does it seem on a world view that crime knows no ideological boundaries and is a recognized problem for planning not only in both simple and complex societies but also in centrally planned and free enterprise societies all along the continuum of values and ideologies.

There has been little to build on, then, for judicious crime prevention, and there have been few means of refining the planning techniques required for

---

[d]Differences between the crime rates of developed and developing countries appear to affirm this—but comparisons of contrasting regions in the same country provided other examples.

crime prevention. So far there has been so little real evidence of specific crime prevention planning that opinions on its most effective implementation still range from a straightforward emphasis on the strengthening of the laws, the efficiency of the police, the increasing of sentences, and the extension of correctional services to the idea of a longer-term and rather pious reliance on better general planning of the economic and social system to eradicate the poverty, discrimination, underprivilege, or injustice from which a great deal of crime undoubtedly flows. Despite centuries of evidence to the contrary, it is still often assumed that people will be better behaved if they have everything they want. Data is accumulating, however, to expose these oversimplifications. Millions of dollars spent, for example, on the equipment and extension of law enforcement in the United States have been accompanied by progressive rises in crime rates, especially in the cities, while the most extensive general economic and social planning of the socialist type in the countries of Eastern Europe have far from eliminated crime as a social problem requiring quite substantial investments in the criminal justice systems. Even where crime rates have been reduced, such as in Japan, the result has proceeded more from the persistence of traditional informal controls than from any conscious planning.

Planning to prevent crime has therefore not yet been tried and found wanting; it has been found difficult and not tried.[e] To a great extent this is so because, as yet, no general philosophy, no body of knowledge exists from which a discipline can be built, and few case studies have been made from which the more general principles can be distilled. Indeed crime prevention planning has had a relatively short history. While the twentieth session of the United Nations Social Development Commission was deliberating the problems in 1969, plans were being made for a meeting of criminologists and economic and social planners, which took place in Rome in June of that year. From the U.N. Secretariat Working Paper which I prepared for that meeting and from the proceedings of the meeting itself, there came the material for a special U.N. Secretariat Working Paper which I wrote for the Fourth United Nations Congress on the Prevention of Crime and the Treatment of Offenders, held in Kyoto, Japan in 1970. This outlined the subject and called for greater study and experimentation; but the opportunities for this have been lacking.

Since then the United Nations Asia and Far East Institute for the Prevention of Crime in Japan has held one brief course on the subject. There has also been one short course held at the Cairo National Institute for Social and Criminological Research, and a seminar was organized at the U.N. Latin American Institute in Costa Rica in 1975. Then in November 1975 the United Nations in cooperation with the Australian Institute of Criminology held, at Sydney, Australia, the First Interregional (i.e., Worldwide) Course on the subject for specialists invited from sixteen nations.

By any standards the subject is still inadequately developed, and the

---

[e]With apologies to G.K. Chesterton who once wrote this about Christianity.

purpose of this book is to examine some of the basic issues in the hope of developing more concrete and practical approaches to the subject.

Essentially what is needed for the future is a new type of professional planner with criminological as well as planning expertise. This means ideally a combined course of training covering all the elements of economic and social planning as well as all the criminology necessary for the work required. This implies years of careful study and field work to produce the new specialist. A shorter method involves training criminologists as planners as well as training planners to be criminologists, but this too is no limited task. It requires innovation, model building, and a range of techniques that can be tested and tried so as to be refined over time to help society develop safeguards against future crime.

The development of professional crime prevention planning does not mean, however, to repeat the mistake of setting up planners as just another separate and specialist body concerned more with blueprints and drafts, more with principles and prospects, than with the actual work. The expertise in planning must be filtered down through all levels of criminal justice and economic and social development. An awareness, of an attitude to the criminal potential of future investments, has to be fostered which can raise the pertinent questions of possible crime before, or during, the process of decision-making. A climate of criminological foresight has to be developed for the years ahead.

Meanwhile the whole range of ideas from development and crime prevention to the combination of these in a planning perspective needs both definition and analysis, with a view to laying the foundation for more serious academic and practical work in this relatively new area of human endeavor.

Social Criminogenics

Whatever forms it takes, crime constitutes a dark silhouette cast by the shape of a particular society, and modern crimes were indeed foreshadowed by the economic and social adjustments to earlier human needs.

One of the reasons that stealing is no great problem in a tribal society on the edge of subsistence is that there is really very little to steal. What everyone else may have—a house, a spear, a loincloth, etc.—is readily available for the making. When such people are brought into a money economy and begin buying bicycles, radios, and more durable tools or clothing, the opportunities and advantages of stealing are created. When a feudal society moves into mercantilism, the types of crimes are likely to change, and property crimes tend to become more numerous than personal crimes—reversing the earlier patterns. There cannot be check frauds without checks, bank robberies without banks, or skyjackings without airplanes, and the relationship between shoplifting and supermarkets offers much food for thought. There is a bureaucracy of organized crime that is as ponderous as its legal counterpart.

Crime is no great public issue in a simple, small, relatively static, homogeneous, and competition-free community. It acquires a more serious demeanor as populations grow, mobility increases, and the division of labor is more intricately subdivided. Vengeance killings protect clan integrity, women, and property in nomadic or pre-agricultural communities. Gangs derive from mutual help groups in immigrant countries. Stealing, robbery, fraud, extortion, and false pretenses abound in an acquisitive social and economic system, such as we associate with modern business and industrialization. Black marketeering and back-door influence flourish where socialistic planning imposes quotas, price controls, and consumer restrictions. Malicious damage to crops, stock theft, and crimes of honor emerge where land is the predominant unit of value and where marriages serve to cement and enlarge family holdings. Enclosures of land and dispossession on a large scale preceded, by centuries, the currency manipulations and illegal shifts in economic power with which we have become familiar today; and Schumpeter was fond of referring to banking as having begun with the crime of lending money that the bankers did not possess. This may yet have a modern echo in the way that banks in some countries have fed inflation and bloated credit to a dangerous extent by risky lending from capital markets, from money borrowed from other banks, and from the unregulated Eurodollar market.[1]

Travel was always dangerous, and indeed the perils of travel abroad were probably greater when pirates, brigands, and highwaymen abounded than they are today, despite the muggings and the spectacular (but still occasional) incidents of hijackings. There are changes in scale and methodology, but the close association between the way we live and the kinds of crime we develop has always been obvious. The pattern of the economy determines to a considerable extent the amounts and types of crime likely to be prevalent. It follows then that the transition from one level of production to another will have its effect upon the quality and nature of the crime that one might expect.

Too little attention has been paid to social criminogenics, and we have still much to learn from the way in which any community of people generates, sustains, and fosters its own deviate contradictions as a normal and, in fact, fairly predictable part of its growth, stagnation, or decline. There is always a persistent dialectic of opposites, which we do not have to be Hegelians or Marxists to acknowledge. Leaving out of account altogether the types of individuals who commit crime, their personal problems, and circumstances, we can predict that by changing the economy, the technology, or the style of life we will effect the nature of crime. Further, we may be sure, on the basis of our experience, that if the population grows and industrialization is pursued, then crime will increase and will probably become more serious in character. This is not the same, however, as saying that crime is either caused or eradicated by social or economic change.

Immense sums have been invested in computers, but until the first major computer frauds were committed, little attention had been given to the opportunities they provided for skillfully diverting funds.[2] The simple reporting of information by the news media can be as abused as it can be used, so that in a country plagued by terrorism, the reporting of one offense could be used by the terrorists as a signal to trigger other offenses in other parts of the country. The building of a road does more than invite more traffic; it may change leisure habits, get people working far from home, encourage divisions in families, and make it easier for people to be attacked and robbed. The building of schools in rural areas may increase the urban army of unemployed, which becomes a reserve producer of offenders. The possible combinations of deliberate changes in our lifestyles and consequent crime potential are myriad and fascinating, and mostly they await closer and more detailed study.

We know that, whatever the end product of the social process, whatever the outcome of the conflict and cooperation in the usual struggle for power that shapes our destiny, crime will be a part and indeed a function of our total structure of both attitudes and institutions—and it will always mirror the fundamental issues of political, economic, social, or technological life. Crime is true and faithful to the realities of life, even when these realities have been masked for years by an established elite or distorted by the legal norms surviving from previous generations. For example, a fall in the standards of honesty will be reflected in more stealing from work or more cheating in business, whether or not this is actually prosecuted, and whether or not law enforcement maintains the old concept that in dealing with thieves it is dealing with the abnormal. Similarly, polluters were offenders even before suitable laws could be drafted to deal with them.

The superorganization of modern crime, with its intrusion into legal and respectable forms of extortion as well as its systematic lobbying for favorable legislation, might be comparable in kind if not in degree to the usury and thinly legalized excesses of some local barons in the Middle Ages. In those days usury was illegal, yet it was practiced and condoned at the highest levels of society by those who had money and those who needed it. Similarly, the poorer people were often cheated of their land by the more powerful and unscrupulous. Neither the usury nor the excesses could have existed without official conniv- ance; both were typical of their economic structures, and both were difficult for the criminal justice system alone to control.

There has been some interest of late in the extent to which crime is created by law and, therefore, in the need for decriminalization, law reform, and a less automatic dependency upon law for the control of behavior. Strangely, this has not extended to the study of the way in which crime situations are created by educational patterns, by the incentives for young people to follow illegal cultures, by the peculiarities of suburban life, the lack of provision for youthful excitement, the kinds of communities we are either creating or breaking down, and the greater rewards now flowing more freely to popularity (even notoriety) than to quiet integrity.

The impersonalization of much modern crime, whether it be street robbery, price fixing, fraudulent packing, or the illegal programming of computers for gain, is as characteristic of the industrial and urban anonymity of our age as banditry or dacoity is typical of the peasantry and village life from which it often arises. Skyjacking and the taking of hostages exploits the media for its modern effect, just as the criminalization of insulting language is normal for tribal peoples living on the edge of subsistence with a fear of destructive clan disputes. Before independence came to Central Africa, it was occasionally possible to uncover examples of Europeans leading bands of African thieves or burglars in a colonialist version of organized crime. There is also some recent evidence that the forms of white-collar crime in Poland follow the local style of collectivities rather than the capitalist pattern of companies and corporations. These cultural considerations have been frequently discussed by criminologists, and they do not disappear with the evolution of more widespread, more sophisticated, or more ruthless crime tied to modern technology. Unfortunately the theme has not been pursued in enough detail to enable us to do more to prevent the negative side effects of our decisions on life.

The point is that criminologists have not proceeded far enough from the cultural conditioning of crime to either the effects of induced change on crime or the effects of crime in molding the society. Crime is not only a concomitant of planned investment and organized change but also is itself an agent of change, and this aspect of macrocriminology has attracted neither research nor sufficient theory-building, despite the clues to its role in both political science and philosophy and the accumulation of data on the effects of modern planning.

The Complications of Development

For years, development has been regarded as good for its own sake. Mankind's constant struggle to improve living standards has appeared sufficient justification for obtaining as much as possible for as many as possible—even if there might be attendant problems of disruption and maldistribution. Despite the caveats of nearly all human philosophy, material wellbeing has been equated (in effect, if not deliberately) with happiness and contentment, and there has been a sense of urgency as populations have grown as a result of improvements in medical knowledge and as the pressures on available resources have increased. Also, the more extended culture contacts, the improvements in worldwide communications, and the consequent rise in expectations, especially in the poorer countries, that conditions would, and should, improve have fueled an increasing public demand for development as a process of modernization if not also equalization.

These expectations were not easy to curb. No-one really wants poverty, newly independent, hopeful countries least of all. Poorer countries sought foreign aid and investment to "prime the pump," communist countries curtailed consumer demands to build an infrastructure of heavy industry, and multinational corporations fostered a global capitalism that generated growth but often drew off the benefits. Perhaps only the United Kingdom sought a higher level of social justice by an ambitious series of social security schemes without labor controls and without a primacy of increased production. Yet even there the thinking was more economic than social, and there was still an expectation that a better-managed economy would somehow provide.

The confidence of experts that they had discovered the ways to reduce poverty, increase employment, and help countries to a "take-off" position from which their growth would be self-generating was increased by the vindication of the Keynesian faith in monetary controls and fiscal policies that had helped America and Europe climb out of depression in the 1930s, by the success of the Marshall Plan by which the U.S. helped Western Europe back onto its feet, and by W.W. Rostow's studies of how development had been fostered or had occurred in the countries that had grown.[3] It was encouraged also by what came to be known as the Harrod-Domar model of economic growth, which grew out of the postwar writings of these two distinguished economists.[4]

Faith in the impersonal an almost automatic process took no account of political or other realities. There are always questions of power distribution, allocation of benefits, and assignment of status roles in the new dispensations, which are thought to contribute to economic growth; but these problems were regarded as somehow separate. They were political or social, not essentially economic or developmental. They might have affected the longer-term aims or have been regarded as purely ancilliary to the planning of development, but they were not seen as changing the means, or the needs, for or the necessary process of development. The long-term economic aim remained, i.e., to maximize production and incomes. This is probably still true in most countries worried about unemployment and reduced living standards because of inflation and the disequilibrium in money markets. People still want to get more, keep up living standards, improve education, and have a house, a second car, or a comfortable old age. Poorer countries want better terms of trade, a greater share of existing wealth—and development is still the key. But there is less single mindedness about it these days. There is, in the more recent work on environmental pollution, in the extending political dissension, and in the recrudescence of massive social problems like crime, unemployment, and student or consumer protest, a greater awareness of the need for balance—and for the rethinking of the older tendency to value only that which could be quantified.

There is a greater appreciation now that development is not such an inevitable process; that it is a delicate mechanism; that it can be wiped out by its own negative by-products; that with its realignment of resources, its impact on living styles, and its negative side-effects, development is a more complex process than has yet been fully appreciated. It is now better understood that there is a dynamic of development involving both growth and change—not only politically and economically but physically, biologically, socially, psychologically, and culturally. Even these broad terms, however, are no more than generic labels for a vast range of ripple effects—of subtle and significant transformations and adjustments that take place at all community and individual levels when the existing order is pushed or disturbed by any deliberate investment in the means of production or in their organization and location. Some of these changes are sequential, compensatory adaptions, but others are disfunctional reactions that gather momentum and that, over time, can serve to negate or emasculate development, frustrating its objectives and leading to greater injustice and unhappiness.

The real costs of development are most evident in the more economically advanced countries where the process of development, with or without planning, has had time to reveal its true colors—both light and dark. But the increase of investments in health, education, and directive government in the developing nations, where planning has been usual, has already congested central areas and created problems with serious political as well as social dimensions. Unfortunately there is no built-in mechanism in nature, society, or people that serves automatically to restore a balance when there is more radioactive fallout, an increase in stifling carbon dioxide in the atmosphere, a growth of ghettos, a dispoilation of forests, a dissipation of community values, and atomization of personalities, a recourse to violence as a problem-solving agent, or an exploitation of others by crime or corruption. It takes centuries for insensitive cybernetics or the steel and concrete monstrosities of modern technology to be overgrown by adjustments to human needs, or for the lost human identity and compassion to reassert itself in the efficient, inexorable, antiseptic drive of society into a sterilized space age. However, the very absence of human elements and the complex interdependence of a reliance on automation makes it vulnerable to the unscrupulous wreckers, the modern luddites, or the cultural barbarians of our times. Successful violence begets violence, just as the effective violation of community interest encourages greater selfishness and disregard, which can destroy all the bases for social wellbeing.

Attention today is rightly concentrated on the avoidance of air and water pollution, but there is an equal need to take account of the pervading insecurity and alienation that make a materially improved life hardly worth living—and which are closely associated with crime.

The wonder and achievement of swift, safe air travel becomes a nightmare when hundreds of passengers' lives depend on whether the itchy finger of a hijacker (who may not be sufficiently educated to understand the theory) will puncture the pressurized cabin. An efficient, modern city of millions can be choked with its own garbage, starved by the middle man bringing in the food, and decimated by maniacs pouring poison into its reservoirs. All the comforts in the world obtained by massive development can become abominations if they are not protected from the wreckers and those motivated entirely by self-interest. What is the use of an air conditioned, perfectly designed, and luxurious bungalow in a jungle exposed to elemental violence and deadly animals. Are people to make fortunes only to pay ransoms or to develop inventions only for abuse. Are laborers to sweat in the fields for the benefit of the idle, who threaten to maim them or destroy their furniture or attack their wives and families if they do not share their wages with the extortionists. These are the realities of life today in a number of countries where there has been too much concern for improvements in material conditions and too little attention given to the social context within which the investments in development were occurring.

This is not to suggest that development should cease or that investments in better material conditions should be reduced—only that they need to be balanced with all costs and benefits, calculated as far as possible in advance. It is not to attack development but to call for more carefully planned development and less reliance on criteria that has now been outmoded by experience. It is to suggest that development be improved by a more extensive use of the criminological knowledge that is available.

Even the communist countries, which have placed most reliance on the central planning of all aspects of the economic and social system, are aware that where alcoholism or juvenile delinquency grows, it is a lack of balance in the planning rather than a fault in the planning itself. At international conferences they are quick to controvert any suggestion of a causal tie between development and crime, because they can produce figures for decreasing crime (as compared with prerevolutionary times), which they attribute to intelligent planning. Yet, even in these countries, there are urban problems of no small dimensions, so that they also need criminal justice services and are well aware that unbalanced planning can have negative effects. And even these countries have still not, as a rule, singled out crime as an area for any specialized planning attention. They still expect it to be amenable to the beneficial fallout of successful general development.

The Rationale for Planning

There is nothing either mystical or recondite in the idea of planning in advance for crime prevention. To some extent it is already being done when budgets are prepared for new police stations or training centers, for improved or extended court houses, or for larger or different types of prisons. Planning for crime has always been implicit in the more general investments in economic growth or in health, education, housing, and welfare investments aimed at producing a healthier, better informed, more highly developed and balanced populace with greater maturity. It is contained in economic and social planning generally. The elements of conscious planning are also discernible where there has been programmed budgeting in criminal justice and other crime prevention services that have developed short-term and long-term objectives.

So far, however, these projections have been intuitive and unsystematic. Often indeed they are unrelated to each other, so that additions to the police or changes in police policy might be beyond the capacity of the courts or corrections. Sometimes, changes in the correctional policy or in court systems have increased the work of the police. However, to take the wider view, health investments have imposed new burdens on education and ultimately on the labor market—and both of these on those trying to prevent crime. The prevention of crime may have been a kind of longer-term policy inherent in these uncoordinated efforts, but it has not been recognizable as such. There is hardly any evidence of research findings having been incorporated in such decision-making. And there has never been a coordination of such arrangements with broader planning for improved health or educational services, new industrial estates, or residential areas. The fact that public investments in agriculture, industry, and commerce have determinable criminogenic features, i.e., they create new opportunities for crime and greater difficulties for the police, and others trying to deal with crime has not been directly linked to any of the provisions for crime prevention services. Nor does it seem that population projections, with future changes in age groupings and the known propensities for crime in certain cohorts, have been used systematically to calculate future needs in crime prevention, as, for example, they have been used to plan for health or education requirements. Even the flow of legislation has not been adequately incorporated into planning for the future needs of crime prevention services. The market research for a new product or a rise in prices is still infinitely more sophisticated than the attempts made to gauge the effects of a new law.

The rationale for planning crime prevention therefore is, first of all, to delineate the area of concern and then to attempt the introduction of system and coordination where, until now, these have been conspicuous by their absence. Second, the intention is predicated on the obvious value of using past experience for future improvement. There is quite obviously enough accumulated knowledge of past mistakes for a refinement of future approaches to the problems of crime. The consequences of urban drift have been ascertainable, as indeed have the bases for projections in nearly all the sectors of planning—except in dealing with crime. The oversight in using these can be explained only by the prevailing but unjustified confidence (to which reference has already been made) that longer-term planning for the economic and social requirements of a society would automatically take care of the more immediate problems of crime and deviancy in general. Too often the immediate problems of unemployment, crime, and corruption have served to undermine longer-term planning and reduce the most carefully devised plans to dust and ashes. Too often a richer society has proved to be more delinquent than poorer and simpler communities.

The best argument for planning, however, is consideration of the intellectual poverty of the alternative. The alternative to planning for crime prevention is the continuance of the disorganized, uncoordinated, ad hoc, and fundamentally crude anticipations of future requirements, which have already characterized the development of the criminal justice services to date without any particularly encouraging results. It is to perpetuate the quixotic hope that crime will take care of itself once the economic and social sinews have been strengthened. In some countries these illusions have already been convincingly shattered by a rising tide of more serious crime, which vastly increased resources for the traditional crime prevention services have been unable to prevent. People are paying dearly in ever increasing taxes to obtain a safer and more just society, to have the freedoms they cherish, and to be unmolested by street criminals or the abusers of power. In the parts of the world where they are paying most, they appear to be getting least value for their money. And it would appear that the more that is spent in the traditional ways to deal with the problem, the lower is the return in terms of safety for citizens and justice for all. Few countries can claim any encouraging degree of success in preventing crime in the older way, i.e., without planning. Merely to state the alternative is, therefore, to make a powerful case for trying to do better.

Any collection of data for better planning can only be an improvement on the past. Any programmed attempt to try out and evaluate different approaches has the advantage of being an improvement of the work done to date. Any conscious preparation for the year 2000, with its foreseeable crime problems, is a step in the right direction. Any work on developing planning tools for the conscious reduction of future crime means a recognition that crime is a serious problem not readily amenable to general and less specific allocations of available economic and social resources. In short, any move in the general direction of a deliberate attempt to prevent crime by improved social and economic adjustments is a distinct contribution to the movement for a better quality of life for all.

The Planning Concept and Its Roots

In outlining the arguments for planning crime prevention, the essential meaning of planning has been revealed. Discussing what it has done or tried to do indicates to a great extent what it is. It is useful, however, to examine planning's prospects and to see how they arose and what they were expected to do. To begin with, it is instructive to consider what others have conceived planning to be—whether for crime prevention or for development generally.

The Concept of Planning

Planned change of any kind suggests theories put into practice and the application or use of acquired knowledge. As Robert Gilpin has said:

The scientist's quest for certainty and his confidence that reason and new methods can solve man's problems are reinforced by his conviction that something which is theoretically possible is also most likely to be politically possible.[5]

The twentieth century has seen an explosion in the technological achievements of man which has raised expectations that he should be able to do something similar with his society.

In planning change in society, the idea is to transfer the usefulness of the physical and natural sciences in producing machinery and devices for the improvement of methods to the social sciences or the behavioral sciences; the idea is that they should do for social relationships what the other sciences have done with and for natural relationships. While most of the planning has been done in the sphere of economics, the planning process is more general and can be applied in a variety of other situations.

Planning has been variously described as:

(a) . . . an organized, intelligent attempt to select the best available alternatives to achieve specific goals.[6]

While this is general, it has a distinctly economic ring to it, because economics itself may be defined as "the allocation of scarce resources between alternative uses." The association is understandable since the economists have had a virtual monopoly in this field.

(b) . . . a . . . process of organized human activities with a view to achieving conscious and systematic adjustments between aims and means and more specifically between expenditures and resources. Planning is therefore focused on two principles . . . coherence (decisions should be compatible with each other and consistent with available resources) and efficiency (no means should be selected if there is a more effective one to achieve a given objective).[7]

This is less exclusively economic and has the advantage of identifying coherence and efficiency as the basic principles of planning—economic, social, or more specifically, crime preventative.

(c) In its generic sense planning is a method of decision-making that proposes or identifies goals or ends, determines the means or programs which achieve or are thought to achieve these ends, and does so by the application of analytical techniques to discover the fit between ends and means and the consequences of implementing alternative ends and means.[8]

In a national sense this means that planning is a process of systematically mobilizing resources in the service of objectives that have been selected by the planning or ruling authorities.

(d) Planning should be seen as a manifestation of the ever growing tendency consciously to organize human activity . . . a continuous search for efficiency in its broadest sense.[9]

Planning then belongs to an older tradition of raising mankind to levels once thought entirely out of reach; and as the past shows, there has been, and sometimes there still is, an air of pretension about national planning, which has ignored human experience with the same assiduity that it has maintained in its appeal to reason. The vicissitudes of the past 30 years have done much to dissipate this confidence; but drawing together the resources of a whole country and then applying them over an entire population to stimulate and sustain growth for a generation or more is indeed a lofty, even godlike, occupation. It is even more exalted than ruling or governing because there is both power and creativity, postulated through a series of changes politicàl, social, and economic. No matter how much planning may be necessary, therefore there is an increasing and corresponding need for more humility about the process than has usually been manifest. A Washington official once remarked that he was puzzled by the way historians could be so uncertain about their analyses of the past, while economists could be so certain about their forecasts for the future.

The other definitional danger we should note is the temptation to present the process of planning as internally consistent and therefore valuable in its own right—whether or not it happens to have any effect upon the real situation in the country or the world:

Attention is directed to the internal qualities of decisions or to the procedures used in making them and not to their external effects.[10]

This builds in a self-protective shield for the professional planner; if the objectives are achieved, then the planning has succeeded. If the objectives are not achieved, it is because society did not comply with planning require-ments—or the resources were not available.[11] If everything goes well, the decision-making was both coherent and efficient; (see definition (b) above) but if something goes wrong, it can readily be ascribed to a lack of compatibility between decisions or to the choice of a means that was not the most effective. The temptation to argue *post hoc ergo propter hoc* is too great—which accounts for the overconfidence of so many planners. They have defined their role so as to make it impervious to evaluation. But in fair terms, a planner should be judged by results not justifications.

The Roots of Planning

Allowing for this, however, we have also to acknowledge that we are dealing here with a brand of pretension that seems to be almost second nature not only to planners, but to people everywhere.

Traditional societies subsist in the hope and expectation that things will not change—that they will be able to depend on the imperatives they have been reared to know and respect. They pray for this, and they prepare for the expected, not usually for the unseen.[12]

More open, progressive societies work hopefully for continuous expansion, embracing change as a challenge and an opportunity for which they need to be prepared. Families build homes for posterity; and individuals, especially when young, often behave as if there were no death; only insurance companies are geared for a calculated disaster.

People plan for the future, therefore, taking as much account as they can of the need to reserve something for the rainy day. Countries have been doing the same thing since Joseph in Egypt and the rulers of Greece and Rome stocked granaries against famine. The hoarding of gold or the more recent acquisitions of property or works of art as hedges against inflation may also be seen as expressions of planning in that they were, and are, provisions for an uncertain future—although these latter examples are a result of an insecurity engendered by the demonstrated incapacity of national planning to insulate the individual from the vaguaries of a fickle fortune.

It is indeed only in recent years that there has been any widespread confidence in aggregate planning, whether regional or national. When the pressures of population were not so disturbing, when incomes were low and hands scarce, feudalism plotted to preserve the status quo by depending upon inheritance and heredity to build local, as opposed to national, security. Families were enlarged, developed, and endowed to provide for themselves through the generations—and this can still be observed in peasant societies. By contrast, the complacent nineteenth century espoused laissez faire as a balance of benefits in a selfish world. Organized national planning was interference with an internal social mechanism and could only disrupt a process of market correctives. The role of government was to provide for defense and order—to hold the ring for the political economy to assert its dynamism in a plethora of self-interest.

It was the 19th century injustice and inequality, the misery and desperation of populations crowded into growing towns, unplanned, unprovided for, unhealthy, unhoused, and discarded, that evoked not only a compassionate philanthropy but a spirit of utopian thinking, social reform, and sometimes revolution. The "beautiful and immutable laws of political economy" by which men sought their "common economic good" did not seem to provide for the poor and weak.[13] Society, if more organized and directed, could surely do better.

The interest in national planning can be traced back to the Enlightenment and Napoleonic times, but it belongs more particularly to the Industrial Revolution and the concurrent increase of population, which brought pressures on the means of production, piled people into factories and hovels, denuded the countryside of labor, and revealed a new countrywide interdependence of demand and supply. All this suggested to some that a better national organization of resources and their allocation might have advantages. This was most evident to Friedrich List who, in Germany and the U.S.A., advanced ideas on national systems, which not only inspired Bismark to unify Germany economically but also fueled the Japanese with systems for their Meiji Restoration and later provided both Lenin and Hitler with the principles upon which their 4-and 5-year plans were based.[14] It was List who pioneered the idea of social overhead capital (especially transportation) as a precondition of economic growth. However, it was Rathenau who organized the first planned national economy for Germany in the 1914-1918 war and gave impetus to the practice of seeking a nationally coordinated operational approach to the political, social, or economic ends in view.

List challenged the classical economists with his organic doctrine of production and the need for a publicly provided infrastructure. Auguste Comte and the Positivists believed human beings could, by asking how instead of why, learn the secrets of nature and create a just and harmonious society. Hegel preached an abstract historicism and the dialectic, which Marx reduced to material terms. From the industrial imbroglio was born a new hope in mankind's capacity to understand and prepare adequately for human needs. A hope that inspired new doctrines of social justice and increased the role of government in protecting the weak from the strong, in taking from the rich to give to the poor, and in redistributing power. Factory laws, minimum wage regulations, trade union statutes, provident funds or pension schemes, health safeguards, child protection laws, and measures to make education compulsory were all ways in which laissez faire was abandoned and governments were brought more directly into the organization of national life. As income tax accumulated and interest groups mobilized, the demands increased for the central governments of free enterprise countries to do more than hold the ring for market forces—to operate, in fact, to provide for the basic minimum of social justice that, it was now realized, a self-balancing, free-market economy could not guarantee. This was still far less than a movement or a policy of comprehensive planning however. A sufficiently powerful and organized political ideology had not yet developed; but after a number of false starts the first *comprehensive* planning system was set up in 1925 by the Soviet Union, and the first 5-year plan began in 1928.[15] In Germany the first Nazi plan covered a period of 4 years from 1933. This coincided with a plan in Mussolini's Italy, with Roosevelt's New Deal, and with a plan for the development of the Tennessee Valley in the U.S. and was followed by a Turkish plan for industrialization.[16]

In general the free enterprise countries regarded such totalitarian-linked approaches as antilibertarian and were suspicious, despite the fact that they had for years been delving piecemeal into the ordering of economic and social life by means of public health, education, social security, and other kinds of legislation. There was, before the Second World War, no great enthusiasm for comprehensive planning, which was often regarded as being counterproductive and self-defeating, not only because of the distortions of demand and supply and the encouragement of black markets but especially because of the bureaucracies that planning procedures were prone to encourage.

Certainly planning had not only been advocated but often loaded with impossible goals. It was expected to provide for everyone in a way that was impossible without such a strict control and extensive direction of labor and labor supply that the constraints on the liberty of people could sometimes mean that whole countries, having dispensed with laissez faire capitalism, began to resemble ideological prisons. The basic needs might be met, but the people had to be satisfied with whatever they were given. There was no unemployment because people were obliged to work to eat, and sometimes they were obliged to fill roles that were not of their choosing. With sufficient power to control the movement of people, oblige them to work, and ration their food and wages, planning can be organized like a prison system, productively, cheaply, and sometimes profitably, but this does not by any means necessarily satisfy those at work. The extremes of planning were sometimes so bureaucratically stifling that opposition to them grew. In the period before the Second World War the cause of free enterprise received a second breath and new blood. Planning was typical, after all, of the totalitarian countries of the left and right. It was not thought to be particularly compatible with a democracy of individual rights and liabilities.

Oddly enough, it was the countries most disenchanted with the authoritarian, totalitarian regimes and their comprehensive planning procedures that were the ones most heavily pressured to adopt more extensive planning schemes in order to mobilize for war against the totalitarians. Perhaps the first examples of such broad based planning in the free enterprise countries occurred in the United Kingdom during the war, when the Economic Section of the Cabinet prepared national product estimates,[17] and when manpower, food, and production were all centrally controlled.

Indirectly then, a degree of national planning achieved respectability in the West and was greatly augmented by the use of similar techniques in Europe to ensure postwar reconstruction. The Marshall Plan and the Organization of European Economic Cooperation were matched by national planning efforts in a number of the countries of Western Europe. At the same time there was an increase in the amount of legislation for medical benefits, social security, welfare housing or industrial regulation. The control of contracts, trade practices, and monopolies was also the subject of legislation so that in effect, the life of the ordinary citizen was more and more subjected to national direction. Yet limitations were frequently drawn to safeguard the citizens' liberty of choice. Large private enterprises flourished, cartels and monopolies developed, and countries were divided on nationalization issues—so that there was, and still is, a very wide gap between the ideas of planning in the West and the comprehensive national planning favored by Eastern Europe and the centrally planned economies. In the communist group the commitment was still to complete public ownership of the basic means of production and State direction and control for the purpose of achieving economic goals, such as the development of more heavy industry. To this end, consumer interests were often postponed, and people were sent wherever necessary to serve the cause.

Although there are still great differences between total planning with all or nearly all sectors public and planning for a wide range of private sectors, there has emerged over the years a gradual but more realistic accommodation on both sides. Centrally planned economies have sometimes relaxed their controls, modified their emphasis on heavy industry, provided for consumer goods, kept real wages attractive, and permitted a measure of private ownership and scope for the profit motive—all, however, within the limits of comprehensive planning. On the other side, free enterprise has been progressively curbed and restrained in countries that had originally rejected central planning. A particularly interesting development has been the adoption of long-range systematic planning by the large companies in the West—especially the multinational companies. They have often gone much farther than their governments and evolved very sophisticated techniques.

A vast range of experience in planning has arisen from the adoption of national plans by the Third World. Countries achieving independence since 1945, with the success of the Marshall Plan in mind and encouraged by Keynesian models of fiscal control, the Harrod-Domar models of economic growth, and the Rostow concept of the stages of development, have sought to promote national growth and economic independence by a kind of planning that is as comprehensive as possible and still consistent with a measure of choice for the private sectors. Sometimes they have gone beyond this and have nationalized the larger industries, banks, or utilities.

The interdependence and complexity of world societies has made general planning a necessity. Emil Lederer writing on the subject of national economic planning in 1933 observed, " . . . the direction of modern society would seem to be toward a planned economy."[18]

The ramifications of a complicated modern, industrial, technological society are such that planning is a kind of basic traffic control or regulation to prevent either chaos, undue hardship, or exploitation. It may not always be well done, and there are times when it benefits some groups or interests more than others. But planning has to be attempted if the myriad activities and decisions are not to conflict impossibly.

At the other end of the continuum, simple societies are poor societies, untroubled by the confusion and interdependence of the large cities—but too poor to permit any wastage of resources. Here planning is necessary for making the best use of scarce or perhaps borrowed resources—or for "priming the pump"—to initiate growth and promote progress to a higher level of production. Here material improvements become important in dealing with population growth and the need for survival. A contented society on the edge of subsistence can hardly remain contented when hit by natural disaster or faced with starvation because of a population explosion beyond available food. Therefore, as it begins to husband its resources and apply them, it is planning.

Finally, the interdependence of society, with its advantages and liabilities makes some form of planning a necessity. Exports and imports, trading terms, and common currencies, whether these refer to international or intranational relationships, make planning of some kind a real need. The dependence of the city on its hinterland and the rural areas on urban trade outlets—and the dependence of both of these on the relationship between capital and labor— enjoin care in the organization of future development; and this usually implies planning.

The complicated progress of development throws up, therefore, its own side effects—many of which could not possibly have been foreseen, but many of which could. It is this latter group that commands attention; and crime is included in that group. Crime is one of the problems about which enough is already known to allow far more realistic forecasting and prevention than has yet been considered.

Levels and Extensions of Planning Concepts and Their Application

It is always necessary when using a word like *government* to be clear about whether central or local government is intended. *Management* can mean anything from the management of an entire industry to the management of a small workshop. And when discussing the *environment*, we need to know whether we are referring to the earth's in the context of outer space or to the immediate conditions of simple cell formation. In all these cases the same principles may apply, but the dimensions of the concept affect and may alter the meaning. So too with *planning*. It is a word that can be used broadly or narrowly. It can be applied to the planning of a nation's economy, to a new city, or to the planning of a playground.

It will be evident from what has gone before that there are many different levels, dimensions, and perspectives from which planning can be conceived; and in order to be meaningful, it is necessary to ensure that these are clear when the terms are used. Comprehensive planning, national planning, programming on a countrywide scale (to include all Ministries, and project formulations of a sectoral or intersectoral nature), have been discussed already. However, it is equally permissible for any single ministry to discuss *its* programs within these plans and to organize *its* projects. All these taken together may be little more than a program for the wider national plan, but under the microscope they assume proportions that allow them to borrow the terms used by the national plan.

It is no less possible for a part of a ministry or a local office or even a voluntary body to make plans and to program for their implementation. Conversely, even beyond the national boundaries, it is conceivable that there be international plans, international programs, and interstate projects. In discussing planning therefore, it is always important to be quite clear as to the levels and extensions of the concepts.

By the same token, the introduction of area concepts of planning like *regional planning* or *zonal planning* or the application of planning concepts to functions, such as *environmental planning* or *crime prevention planning*, admit of interpretation in terms of "plans, programs, and projects" but in a sense somewhat different from that which has been used in this book so far. Nevertheless, it should not be thought that this variation in the possible levels on which planning, programming, and project-making can be conceived changes in any way the basic approach. The model remains. The varied contexts, extensive or intensive, affect only the significance and application of the planning. We can plan for an empire or a household by use of the same principles, but the significance of the terms used will be different; and it will not always be possible to apply them in exactly the same way.

All these efforts to highlight special areas or special programs for a planning approach interfere in no way, therefore, with the basic principles already outlined above. The distinction of scale is necessary to avoid confusions and misunderstanding by ensuring that the levels and functions are clearly defined. However, it is obvious that the basic techniques of collecting data, decision-making, allocation of resources, the setting of priorities, the determining of objectives, the selection of benchmarks, and the evaluation of programs all belong to a distinct methodology—an approach to development or to a problem-solving matrix that can be used at every stage and every level. Just as mathematical principles can be applied to the minutiae of an atom or the apparently limitless extensions of space, so planning has its own technique, its own logic or way of thinking, which can be applied at the village level, the international level, or any of the intermediate stages. A single project in a very large international plan could itself be the total plan for a single country and, in this other scene, could have its own programs and projects. On the other hand, a simple project for a new school or new hospital can be regarded as the total operation for planning, with its own plan showing the aims, and objects, the allocation of resources, and the timetable; with its own programs of construction and operation and its own specific projects for special operating theatres, language laboratories, gymnasia, X-ray equipment and intercommunications, and so forth.

Planning is not only a process, therefore, but a way of thinking that can be applied in a macro or microfashion—and, as we have seen, in its essentials it is not unrelated to what most people try to do in providing for their own households now and in the future. This is at once the source of its value, and sometimes the fount of its confusion.

Criminal Justice And The Other Sectors

It is difficult for anyone unaccustomed to thinking of intersectoral planning to see at once the connection between crime and agriculture, crime and local government, or crime and, perhaps, industry or labor. These are in most countries enormous areas of separate concern with their ministries and policies that sometimes seem remote from crime prevention and criminal justice. Indeed to those preoccupied with these other ministries or sectors it may seem rather like special pleading to intrude the criminal concept into their domains. Crime is thought to be for the police, the courts, and corrections to handle, and it is not something of particular or direct interest to the productive structural or specialist departments. The modern developmental criminologist does not think this way. Crime is a feature, perhaps an inevitable feature, of social life. To prevent it or control it we have to look to society itself.

It may be trite to say that human nature and social relations cannot be divided between those who are paid to deal with crime and those who aren't. However, crime, no matter how it is defined, is concerned with behavior, and criminal behavior knows no sectorial boundaries. Indeed the criminal justice services are often dealing with problems created, neglected, or promoted by action, or the lack of it, in the other sectors of the economy. We readily appreciate that it would be nonsense to leave health entirely to doctors or legislation to lawyers. Education is too broad to be confined to the idea of formal classroom education. Yet, with the exception of pleas for community support or public involvement, we are still prone to leave crime to the specialists. Its intrusion into the routine work of education, health, welfare, industry, forestry, agriculture, and government itself attracts too little attention. Thinking of planning crime prevention intersectorally or cross-sectorally, however, involves us in a consideration of these wider perspectives.

Agriculture and Crime

Crime is not usually a great problem in rural areas, where communities are small and social life is so integrated that social controls are strong. But from a planning point of view, agriculture is certainly an area with criminogenic potential. Often, in the process of planning, large sums of money are devoted to the improvement of agricultural production—and there are a number of developing countries that will be predominally primary producers until at least the end of this century. The simple expedient of making such large sums available can itself attract unworthy attention. Government money offered as loan funds for seed purchase or the improvement of equipment or stock can attract crime. Apart from the prospects of embezzlement or mismanagement of the funds themselves, there is the possibility of fraudulent applications, illegal use of the money, or exploitation of the application rights of others.

In one African country the World Bank made millions of dollars available for cooperatives and to encourage small-scale farming. There were many failures of cooperatives, some followed by prosecutions for embezzlement or theft but some just tolerated as mismanagement. This occurred at a time when the handling of money as distinct from goods and the procedures for earning a wage, budgeting, and saving were all relatively new to rural Africans in this particular area. They were not accustomed to managing cooperatives, and they defaulted—more from inexperience in dealing with accounts than from venality. However, in this investment cooperative production did not make much headway, and a number of people were labelled as criminal who might have been spared the experience.

Incidentally, the same planning decision to put money into small farming could find few outlets in the large agricultural areas for which it was intended. However, both ministers of government and public servants rushed to purchase weekend properties, which qualified them for the funds available. Technically justifiable, the obtaining of funds for this kind of part-time, sideline farming by people already well provided for by the system was a diversion from the original purposes. No doubt deeper investigation would have uncovered the kinds of deception and even corruption that an ill-considered investment had encouraged.

The peasantry and taxation has traditionally been an area for despoilation, deception, concealment, and deceit. A portion of crops has frequently been taken by governments, and large expropriations have been a feature of rapacious governments. Conversely, it has frequently been customary for the farmers to conceal crops, make false returns, dodge taxation when possible, and seek to qualify for subsidies rather than be liable for tax. With the rise of "agrobusiness" in many countries, the amounts involved could be very considerable. Perhaps it should be added that such benefits from subsidies or exemption from tax have customarily been bought in many countries by the bribing of the appropriate officials.

Where there are national systems for the control or organization of agricultural production, there is often an incentive to supply a black market or evade crop collections by authorities. This was a characteristic of the Kwangtung farmers response to the grounding of China's Great Leap Forward in late 1950s and into 1960.[19] Similar situations arose in wartime England when food production was controlled and food rationed. It has happened in Russia, is almost a tradition in France, and is a situation well understood in most agricultural areas It is easy to see, therefore, how certain government policies can be criminogenic. They can make farmers into offenders to maintain living standards, or they can encourage evasions of thoughtless or unworkable laws to supplement the wrong agricultural policies.

From another angle, there was a time when the farmers of one West Indian country would not grow crops because of crop stealing. As soon as crops ripened they were stolen. It was also customary in Cyprus for farmers to put their beds out in their fields at harvest time, not only because the weather was hot, but to discourage thieves. In such circumstances effective crime prevention can be a contribution to agricultural production.

Again, it is only possible to touch here upon the vast problem of double-dealing and exploitation in land. Over the centuries the conditions of tenure, the concentration of holdings, and the provisions for dispossession or disinheritance have formed a sorry story of dishonesty and aggrandizement. The line between legal and illegal action has not always been easy to draw. Further, it has been even more difficult to explain to unfortunate people who may have lost their possessions because they were too poor to use the law and too uneducated to appreciate what was happening to them. Moreover, from such problems of possession and dispossession have sometimes flowed the motives for arson, assault, and even murder. History offers many examples of banditry as a reaction by the underprivileged to dispossession and exploitation.[20]

In the same context, the opportunities for crime in the supply of farms with their seed, tools, equipment, and perhaps their upkeep until the harvest is reaped or in the buying and marketing of their produce have their corollaries in overseas trade or inducement for changing land use. There is an area of overlap between sharp dealings and criminal conduct, but the possibilities for crime are demonstrated if only by the relatively few cases of illicit transactions that come to light. Nor can the possibility of defalcation either by the farmers in valuations or the middleman in price-fixing or monopolizing (where this is illegal) be overlooked. These are all openings for crime that a system can provide and the most vigorous policy cannot easily prevent. In fact they often have an offshoot in the corruption of officials.

The point is that there are ways of planning for better and more productive agriculture without creating quite so many opportunities or incentives for crime. Crime prevention in this area would logically include accountability at all stages of a program of agricultural improvement to ensure the best and most honest returns to the funds invested, to keep out the unscrupulous operators, and to ensure a fairer and more secure deal for the farmers themselves. This is an aspect of crime prevention of special interest to those countries most dependent upon farming. Great punishment, threatened or visited upon the delinquents, or vast extensions of police forces to intensively control rural areas are usually difficult or impractical; and they are not nearly as effective as an intelligent revision of the system so as to make better use of those existing social controls that already serve to prevent a lot of housebreaking and robbery in the country districts.

There are some areas of the world where the connection between agriculture and crime is more direct and obvious. Cattle thefts abound in some Masai areas of Africa, because Masai tribesmen have believed in the past that all cattle belonged to them. Rustling in the old cowboy film tradition makes the point very clearly. The adulterating of products to get better prices at the market has a long history in the annals of business acumen, fraud, or sharp practice.

Vengeance crimes, e.g., the burning of a neighbor's crops or direct violence to repay a wrong, are outgrowths of property concepts and standards of behavior in rural areas. Investments in production might also incorporate consideration of the possibility of aggravating such situations by perhaps increasing the possibilities of unequal or unfair treatment or the exploitation of one group by another.

A good deal of what is written below about the connection of crime with industry, commerce, and business is repeatable in the agricultural area. Indeed the mechanization of farming and the introduction of business methods have made it difficult sometimes to draw a clear line between industry and agriculture. Farmers have a need for law and order to produce: the middlemen services offer tremendous opportunities for the unscrupulous to exploit both the producer and consumer—a fact that has not escaped organized crime syndicates; and in the lobbying for government grants, subsidies, and supports, there is a line beyond which corruption quickly asserts itself.

A final link between crime and the agricultural sector is the extension of the criminal label. This might well be broadened by agricultural policies calling for tariffs and quotas, price or wage regulations, and penalties for not obtaining appropriate licenses for land use, animal health, or the import of equipment or materials. This extended use of the law to achieve economic or social change or to effect administrative shifts of emphasis in agriculture may either be difficult to implement—so that the law is honored in the breach and more people are technically offenders but in fact hardly ever prosecuted— or it may be overused so that people who should be ploughing the land or harvesting the crops are likely to overcrowd the prisons. Either way the law is being abused. Also the plan for the agricultural sector is likely to be distorted by the improper use of the law and the extension of its criminal creating potential.

Industry, Commerce, and Crime

In a report to a U.S. Senate Select Committee on Small Business Administration one facet of the crime-business problem was presented, but business can generate as well as suffer from crime.

This report makes it plain that thievery and vandalism have reached such proportions that survival of the small businessman in high crime areas has reached the crisis point. . . . It shows graphically the deep impact crime is having on the small businessman whose losses are proportionately thirty-five times greater than those sustained by big business.[21]

No reading of history could possibly overlook the close relationship between the legal and illegal in both business and industrial growth. One wonders why then there is often such surprise at finding some of the more enterprising criminal syndicates investing their ill-gotten gains in legitimate enterprises and then using some of the familiar tricks of the trade (like undercutting prices to squeeze out or take over competitors, then fixing prices of their own making) to obtain higher profits and extend their empires. Many of the most powerful and respectable financial organizations have had their origins in questionable practices—and it used to be said that one must not ask a millionaire how he made his first million! Greed and avarice are particularly evident where wealth is concentrated. Therefore, the planning, financing, and development of plant, factory, chains of retail outlets, and the like, not to mention the concomitant stock exchange dealings, usually offer immense scope for the sharp witted and unscrupulous.

It will be quite unnecessary to dwell here on the crime potential of stock, share, and commodity exchanges. The fact is that Security and Exchange Commissions have had to be set up in many countries to deal with the unscrupulous and fraudulent use of exchanges. The great swindles from the South Sea Bubble of the 18th century, the floating of questionable holding companies in our own times, and the globalization of oligopoly capitalism with its power over prices and wages[22] are just a few of the indicators that, in this market, the laws can and are being breached or circumvented to a degree dangerous to any economy. The fact that in this kind of economic activity so very much depends upon trust is indicative of the scope for false pretenses and of the danger of business confidence being undermined by venality and bad faith. Opportunities for restrictive trade practices, the creation of monopolies to control both supplies of raw materials or prices, the complications of control introduced by the modern process of interlocking directorships, and the increasingly dominant share holding of pension funds, trusts, insurance companies, mutual funds, and holding companies provide a background for crime against consumers which few modern societies have been able to cope with. The ramifications are extensive. Ryan has given an example of the failure of one of the largest financial institutions in Canada (because of criminal fraud), which affected confidence in the financial market and may have contributed to a half percentage point rise in the country's interest rates.[23]

These forms of trading and management should be areas of intense concern to any planner, since the meaning and implications of his data as well as the reach of his projections can be nullified by manipulations of company stock and dilutions of credibility on the national exchanges. More important, the benefits of planning can be skillfully diverted, not only to the undeserving, but out of the country. This is a specialized area, however, in which a crime prevention planner needs either to be skilled—or to know how to draw on the necessary skills—if he is to advise on the ways to counter the efforts likely to be made to divert funds to illegal uses or to pockets for which they were never intended.

Similarly, special skills may be needed to provide the advice that planners are increasingly going to need to forestall the activities of economic criminals, whether these be within the multinational corporations or independent operators acting as opportunities beckon. The various devices for evading customs duties, price controls, and import or export restrictions are obvious snares for any plan to avoid if it is not to be financially decimated at an early stage.

At the national and international levels, the concept of economic crime has become increasingly important, particularly in the relationships between developed and developing countries. Countries getting nowhere in their attempts to organize development have sometimes realized that benefits were being syphoned off by companies manipulating the pricing externally and internally to minimize customs or excise charges and evade foreign exchange controls, by producing in low labor-cost areas and selling at high profit in high labor-cost areas, or by using capital investment to ensure markets for foreign imports. The variations on this theme have been increasing recently—but always seemingly in the direction of benefiting the "haves" against the "have-nots" and using commercial or business ingenuity and the best (albeit the most expensive) legal skill and acumen to circumvent the laws. Occasionally corruption has been resorted to in order to encourage the enactments of laws that extract benefits from the people for whom the benefits were originally intended.

While the idea may be unpopular in some quarters, it is only fair to observe that the opportunities for crime creation or extension are not to be discovered on only one side of the management-labor equation. A consumer or those intended to benefit from planning for development may be cheated or deprived of rightful expectations by illicit union activities. Investigations of the activities of some leading figures in the labor fields in the U.S.A. have uncovered the use of violence to ensure union membership or support, the use of funds for purposes never intended by members contributing, and some questionable associations of union leaders with known operators of organized crime. Power can corrupt, whether it be political, capitalistic, or labor based. More important for our purposes, it is necessary to look not only at the obstacles to the plan, which the abuses of such power can impose, but at the laws that may be devised to deal with such problems, and perhaps to draft new and more appropriate laws as a part of effective planning.

The large funds that have to be made available for the installation of plants, the movement of labor, and the purchase of equipment all create their own temptations, from the stages at which there may be opportunities for corruption between officials and lenders or negotiators to the frauds or pretenses at the tendering or subcontracting of the electrical, plumbing, or carpentering work to be performed. At the same time the openings for the unfair and illegal exploitation of workers and their families moving into new housing estates have to be anticipated if the plans are to be implemented successfully. There was a time in some of the developing countries when idle and dissolute persons who had infiltrated housing areas (and who had more time to organize simply because they were not working) actually controlled the residents to the point of obtaining protection money (to avoid attack at night, robbery, or the breaking of new furniture) and dictating the use of voting rights. In some areas of the world where superstition or a belief in magic held sway people have been frightened out of their earnings or savings by the threat of a curse or a spell. Industrial investment means not only protection of the funds from diversion and protection of consumers, but also protection of honest workers.

This therefore raises the obvious prospects for crime when people move and in the process either leave behind or neglect the older social controls. It may be difficult for these informal controls to survive in a town if the basic family unit is the extended group, i.e., with relatives as well as the parents and children—and if the housing provided or available takes no account of this. Though it is an extreme example, it is apposite that in an African matrilineal family it is not the father but the mother's brother who is the family authority; he takes the place of the father in a Western nuclear family. But when the parents and children come to town, he is not regarded as part of the family. Of course, he doubtless has his own wife and children to think of, even though it will be *his* wife's brother who will be *their* authority figure. This division of the social-family unit has done much to break the older controls. Similar examples could be given of the dilution of Asian social controls by the movement of only a part of the earlier unit. In the West it has been the vertical responsibility of parents for children, or children for aged parents, which has been allowed to disintegrate and has indeed been encouraged by the types of social security schemes that individualize rights and benefits—sometimes with little or no reference to the natural family unit. These are usually relatable to industrialization and urbanization, and they have always helped to make crime easier to commit and more difficult to detect and inhibit.

Within industry itself, stealing from the firm is sometimes quite endemic. In fact, it has been so prevalent that it might even be discounted in wages offered, e.g., less may be offered because it is assumed a worker will probably steal up to a given amount from his employer. Conversely, such oncosting to wages, or stringent surveillance has sometimes led trade unions to take industrial action to prevent workers from being searched or otherwise incommoded by the tightened security. This is a very necessary area for careful thought when it comes to planning the most productive, cooperative, and competitive industries.

This may be the place to include the criminogenic potential of manipulations of trusts, wills, and executorships. It covers both inheritance and the management of estates, and it refers to agriculture as well as industry. We are concerned here, however, with its property and business management aspects. Clearly, when beneficiaries are cheated, or feel that they have been cheated, out of considerable bequests and perhaps thereby denied advancement or improvements in the social status conferred by wealth, they are likely to react. And sometimes they react violently. There are many examples from countries all over the world, so one should suffice here—written by the offender himself. In the nineteenth century a certain J.F. Mortlock tried to murder both an executor of his father's will and a Fellow of Christ's College Cambridge because he believed himself to have been swindled. He was convicted, and perhaps because of the exalted status of his victims, he was sentenced to be transported to Australia for 21 years. Even when he had served his sentence and returned to England, he continued until his death in 1882 to conduct a campaign with government departments and the Courts for the prosecution of the executor and the return to him of the property.[24] This is by no means an isolated case, and it dramatizes the need for sufficient accountability to be built into equity inheritance legislation—and its implementation. There is the white-collar crime prospect of defalcations by trustees and executors on the one side and on the other the possibility of criminal reaction by the dispossessed (or the person convinced that he has been dispossessed).

In commerce there have been a great many examples of delinquent groups obtaining monopolistic control over supplies or distribution by violence or crime. The transport services are a good example. Here the individual operators can be, and have been squeezed, out of business (if the profits warrant it) by all kinds of illegal, even strong-arm methods. Extortion, arson, and the destruction of goods are other weapons available to the kind of gangs likely to be operating. The purchasing, the wholesaling, and even the retailing end of the business have always attracted the more ruthless and sophisticated criminal groups—which may, however, have achieved respectability over time. Some provision needs to be made—probably especially where the plan is actually succeeding, to make sure that the illegal operators do not take over and divert the benefits of the plan to themselves.

Gambling and money lending have been activities of special interest to organized crime, and even in countries where crime is far from organized in this sense, gambling and money lending remain activities for special attention, if crime prevention is to be attempted. Gambling and money lending may seem to be only on the periphery of commerce, but they are transactions peculiarly suited to the requirements of those with an interest in money and few scruples about how to get it. The fact that they are usually of both interest and service to the poorer classes means that those least likely to be able to afford it are usually the real victims.

There have been far too many examples of the tremendous impact of industry and commerce on lifestyles and behavior generally for there to be any need to stress the criminogenic implications. In our own time not only television, electronics, motor vehicles, airplanes, and the automation of production but also supermarkets, credit cards, computors, refrigerators, processed foods, and the virtual explosion in the servicing sector of the economy have had profound effects on the way people live. Birth control devices, on which enormous industries have grown, and the plastication of births, marriage ceremonies, and especially funerals have sometimes transformed older family occasions into cheap commerce, while tourism, the organization of leisure, the commercialization of Christmas, and the linking of people across vast distances by telephone have changed people's needs and interests in ways that the unscrupulous have not hesitated to exploit illegally.

Man's life is inevitably centered around production, so that when this changes, it affects his home, family, friends, and a wide variety, if not all, of his relationships. The younger people seek more profitable incomes from new forms of industry—and with it the freedom of behavior not always available if they live near their families. Workers and employers, whether capitalist or communist, are likely to find many of their differences centering around the investments in, or the conditions of, production. These have sometimes meant violence, fraud, exploitation, and dispoilation associated with the developments in industry. It is naive for any society to create mass community problems by industrial development or new commercial techniques and then expect to resolve them by means of criminal justice services like the police, courts, and corrections. The consequences both economic and social of industrial and commercial investment are sufficiently well known for a little planning attention to be accorded to new moves in these directions—with a view to reducing the potential for crime. And, if the increase in crime is deliberately discounted because of other advantages sought, then the real cost of the new enterprise to the consumer (e.g., in terms of the higher prices he will have to pay for insurance against crime) must be carefully worked out and made known.

Perhaps a word should be added here about the fact that planning can neither intend to nor have the real power to stifle local protest or legitimate dissent. The extent to which this will be controlled will depend more upon the ideological slant of the country and not so much on the planning. Even crime prevention planning can make full allowance for the venting of protest and opposition, if this is the way in which the law is framed. Naturally, planning can be abused; it can be used for repression. However, neglect of dangers or lack of repression can be used by offenders to tyrannize where there are organized groups ready to take advantage of a totally permissive situation. The degree of tolerance is still being worked out in practice in many of the developing and developed countries committed to individual freedom. And the absence of planning to prevent crime is sometimes highlighted by the extent of the planning to commit crime by well organized crime syndicates or shady business practitioners.

Education and Crime

There was a time when education and crime could be regarded as opposites. We called for more schools and less prisons, the assumption being that the disadvantages or the inequity of criminal conduct would be readily perceived by an educated person and he would therefore seek advancement in more personal and professional fulfillment. It can perhaps still be argued that the right kind of education will be crime preventative, but this only begs the question. What is the right kind of education?

It is indisputable that improvements in the educational system in many countries have been accompanied by rises in the crime rate and that the numbers of young people now held longer by educational institutions have been the power for use in confrontations, which have increased the tasks of the police. On the other hand, in the more serious types of crime, like robbery with violence, rape, etc., it is often the school or university dropout who features most prominently, suggesting that deprivation of legitimate opportunities for achievement contributes to a diversion to illegitimate channels of gain and recognition. However, it is difficult to draw the conclusion that the provision of opportunities alone will solve the problem. There is a link between the lack of legitimate advancement by educational qualifications and crime—but it is more subtle than has, so far, been appreciated. Similarly, it is clear that better and more professionally educated culprits are required to perpetuate the highly sophisticated corporate crime or white-collar crime offenses that have also shown signs of increase.

The subject is indeed vast, and the implications both subtle and ramified. All that can be said here is that care must be taken in educational development to avoid the possible criminal spinoffs. The simple multiplication of teaching institutions and formal qualifications may not be education at all. Quality is no less important. Education may well prove to be the key to the prevention of increased crime—if it is education for life and not for social recognition by diploma gathering. The two are related but are not inextricable.

In any changing society the need to educate for the challenge of change clashes with the need to educate for essential conformity, i.e., in the sense of learning to observe the common decencies by which any society is able to function. It may be that in an attempt to balance these competing requirements, an educational system might fail to provide either the ability to conform or the ability to adapt, and herein lies the root of some of the increases in individual and group crime. By the same token, some of the developing countries have been learning, to their detriment, that irrelevant education, i.e., education for its own sake or for personal fulfillment, unrelated to the realities of life can be disturbing and crime productive. When only a rural livelihood is available in a country but children are trained for service-type or official-type jobs so that they are unhappy with anything else (and perhaps prefer to be unemployed), there is a yearly build-up of a pool of resentment and idleness simply waiting for exploitation. These are but a few of the fundamental relationships between education and crime.

Health and Crime

Once again it seems reasonable to consider that a healthy normal person will not need to commit crime and will have the mental as well as physical strength to resist it. This is an oversimplification, however. Most offenders are indeed normal, and many who get away are above average. Obviously there are links between ill health and crime, which are well documented, whether it be the epileptic or schizophrenic person becoming violent and attacking others or the physically handicapped overcompensating for his disability. By the same token, however, the amounts spent on mental health and preventative medicine have a direct relationship to crime prevention. This was clear in New Jersey in the 1950s when a diffusion of funds to mental health and broader health services generally resulted in a decrease in the allocation for a new prison; the prison was never built, and this led to dissatisfaction for prisoners and penal reformers alike as a result of overcrowding in the old institution in the 1970s.

In developing countries, expenditures on health and the resulting population effects greatly increased the vulnerable youth group and the need for outlets, without which frustration could generate social problems—and possible crime. In developed countries, the very availability of funds means a form of competition between the level of health expenditure possible and desirable and the level of behavior toleration. There is no end to hospital, specialists services and research improvements if these can be afforded, and similarly there is no end to education, court, and police needs if the funds are there. The balancing of these demands is not easy.

The crime it is sought to prevent may be produced by a lack of expenditure on health or education—or by a lack of expenditure on the enforcement of a particular law. There is an interdependence, therefore, between the sectors and a relationship between the forms of planning. At this stage, too little is known about the optimal, or even the most prudent, allocation of resources between these uses. Anyway, it would probably depend upon the objectives. If health were to be the most important objective, then it might be worthwhile tolerating a substantial degree of crime. If crime prevention were to be the major concern, then it might greatly affect the amounts available for both health and education. Clearly, more research is needed to ensure that a balance can be achieved with more precision than could possibly be expected now. Too little is known about criminal behavior to permit more than a rule of thumb allocation at this stage. On the other hand, too little is known about disease and preventative medicine— physical and mental—to allow anything more accurate. Planners are working to a great extent in the dark—listening to experts on all sides and unable to satisfy them all. Usually, however, the crime or crime preventative implications have been ignored.

The United Nations First Interregional Course on Crime Prevention Planning, held in Sydney, Australia in November 1975, made the very valuable observation that in seeking to prevent crime there had been too much dependence upon the criminal justice services and, in this respect, countries might well ask whether the criminal justice field could not usefully find a model for its future from the health field. In promoting good health, it had already been accepted by most societies that social and economic forces could have a much greater impact on health than all the specialist health services combined.

Good eating habits or a better distribution of incomes, better housing, more leisure, etc. could do more to preserve health than all the doctors, nurses, hospitals, and special care units. Similarly, crime prevention would probably benefit more from improved economic and social conditions than from all the increases in prisons, courts, and police services. Law-abiding behavior, no less than health, is a total community issue that cannot be left entirely to full-time experts. But conditions need to be improved with an eye to the criminogenic elements of such investments.

General Observations on Cross Sectoral Planning for
Crime Prevention

Corruption, school drop-outs, employment or educational frustrations, impersonal lifestyles, opportunities for fraud or theft are some of the factors leading to criminal behavior which will often lend themselves to solutions by concerted attacks by all sectors in a national planning operation—not just those services labelled "criminal justice." If health, education, welfare, industry, commerce, agriculture, housing, as well as criminal justice services were to combine to make a coordinated effort to eliminate these criminogenic factors, society would greatly benefit—and so each of the sectors mentioned would be more capable of reaching their objectives with less interference from crime.

Again, these nonspecialist sectors often contribute unwittingly to an unnecessary extension of the criminal label by using punitive laws to enforce compliance with their programs. They have recourse to licensing legislation, which relies upon fines, failure to pay, which could lead to imprisonment. The number of these laws has increased tremendously over the years. This is a criminogenic potential that could well be reduced by greater reliance on public education, re-education, and other less punitive and more constructive approaches.

In all these approaches, the sectors can learn from each other. Specialist criminal justice services could incorporate the elements of the national plan into their training and often could use the research and library or training facilities of the other sectors. Similarly, other sectors could incorporate some of the needs and techniques of criminal justice into their own programs, as for example, in the reduced reliance on law enforcement, the building in of necessary security and appropriate checks for accountability in the handling of funds or the prevention of fraud. All this implies intersectoral committees for more effective studies of the way sectors can integrate, not only to prevent crime, but to unite their efforts to meet common objectives.

Crime Prevention and Physical Planning

The link between crime and the physical conditions in which people live has been established since caves were both homes and hide-outs, since churches provided refuge from the world for the saintly and sanctuary for the outlaw, and since cities nurtured both the enterprise of the Renaissance and the miserable venality of Fagin's kitchen. The types and forms of crime are determined to no small extent by the terrain and its use: by the layout of towns, highways, business centers, and residential areas. Slums, ghettoes, *favellas, bidonvilles*, unauthorized settlements on municipal boundaries, and the inner city decay of some of the larger urban areas today are consequences of physical distributions of buildings, communications, and services.

Robin Hood could operate with relative safety from the forests; highwaymen in the eighteenth century could ply their trade effectively between the towns, villages, and cities because of the absence of security services in the interstices of human settlement; and the quest for privacy in high-rise apartment buildings has cloaked the offender with a convenient anonymity. For generations people lived in walled cities not only to withstand enemy seiges but to provide much needed protection against nighttime marauders. The secret panels, "priest holes," and escape routes built into some of the larger houses had obvious value for evasion of the law. Even the size, design, and strength of the Pyramids were determined, in part at least, by the anticipation of the need for structures to forestall the attentions of grave robbers down the ages.

Cities where policemen patrolled in two's, the crime-ridden warrens of the European towns of the nineteenth century, the "delinquency areas" in town centers described by criminologists in the 1930s, and more particularly the surprise occasioned by the discovery that the new housing estates developed for slum clearance all over Europe had more juvenile delinquency than the collections of hovels they had replaced, all testify eloquently to the close connection between crime and the physical environment. With this kind of background it is difficult to understand why attention has been paid only recently to the criminogenic consequences of urban planning, the physical arrangement of buildings, and the styles of housing. While it has long been recognized that all kinds of social problems are likely to flow from housing people too far away from work and entertainment or from structures which isolate individuals and give them no real sense of belonging or little scope for community life and social improvement, the full impact of housing and neighborhood design on the patterns of human behavior has yet to be fully worked out. Again, the explanation can only be that the concern for satisfying human needs has carried with it an implicit assumption that creature comforts and status, shopping and entertainment facilities, community halls, churches, and business centers will generate the kind of satisfying social life sufficient, in itself, to inhibit crime.

There is, of course, a good deal of truth in this, if the right kind of community interest and cohesiveness can be encouraged by the groupings of residences and facilities. However, this does not go far enough from a crime prevention point of view, and indeed if the past is any guide, there do not appear to be many examples of success in achieving this kind of social cohesiveness in modern urban planning. From the point of view of effective crime prevention, allowance has to be made not only for the frustrations and artificiality imposed by certain physical restraints on styles of living but for the fear and insecurity that is increased by certain types of buildings, amenity placements, and residential lay-outs, for the absence of communications during high-risk periods, and for the complications that certain combinations of roads and buildings introduce into the deterrence, investigation, detection, and treatment of crime. The crime-ridden warrens of some of the major cities of the past were partly so afflicted because they were difficult to police, offered refuge to anyone fleeing the law, and locked into the alien system many people who could not afford to live anywhere else and were afraid to attract attention to themselves. They helped to build up the kind of local community subculture sympathetic to people on the run and antagonistic to the authorities. At the same time, they frequently developed an internal morality and social control of their own that was often destroyed when these slums were cleared and the people were rehoused in physically improved dwellings which gave, however, less immediate contact and forced adaption to more distant and less personally involving relationships. People have a need for safety as well as a need for supplies, education, entertainment, health services, and community facilities. This does not mean simply having police stations handy but encouraging the kind of community interest in each other that makes it difficult for strangers to intrude without challenge or escape without notice. It may mean placing play and recreation areas within the center of housing projects rather than on the perimeter—or the location of residential sites where the flow of people at most times of the day will act as a deterrent to crime.

The most publicized and perhaps significant work on the relationship of crime prevention and urban design is that of the architect Oscar Newman, who discovered interesting differences in crime rates between different types of housing in the city of New York.[25] A great deal more information will be provided by the data that have been, and are being, gathered by the United States Law Enforcement Assistance Administration aided projects, comparing different styles of building and subsequent crime rates. Apart from this, a great deal of thought and attention is given to the location of business premises and centers of all kinds; before building there may be market research or long observation of the habits of residents. But in the location of courts, police stations, and prisons, the sounding of opinion and the projection of needs has been relatively crude. The link of police and public support in the prevention of crime has been particularly neglected in the location of buildings, and few basic precautions have been built in.

The possibilities are immense, but they are not without some complications as the interests of law and order compete with individual rights. For instance, an obvious preventative of crime is more day-to-day surveillance of neighbors—not only for mutual protection but for the discovery of unusual habits that may have a reference to crime. This has been, down the years, a well-tried method of crime control, and it can be aided by physical design. Arranging some houses to overlook others or all houses to overlook public pathways and roads can greatly aid crime prevention.[f]

At some stage, however, the opposing principle of privacy is encountered. While it is obvious that windows overlooking approaches to buildings and public paths make it more difficult to rob someone without witnesses—with the aid of judiciously placed street lighting—and while the provision for the surveillance of residents by placing houses in such a way as to monitor others makes it difficult for occupants to deviate from expected behavior, it is equally true that this promotes intrusion and curiosity to an extent that is dangerous to individual privacy and may, in a subtle way, affect the basic rights to free movement and independence. If both the community need for safety and the individual interest in privacy are to be served, therefore, a delicate balance has to be struck in physical planning and design.

One solution might be to leave the decision to the residents themselves. If people are to be allowed to decide of their own free will whether to live in fish bowl security (i.e., less privacy but more communal safety) or in the greatest privacy, with all the crime risk this may entail, they can perhaps determine for themselves the relative priorities. Much will depend upon the type of social organization that can be developed around the physical designs of residential areas. There is likely to be far less objection to neighborly surveillance if it is to be the natural and unobtrusive observation of a community of people who really care about each other than if it is the intrusive, impersonal, and perhaps critical curiosity of people who live beside each other but who have nothing really in common with each other. It is usually a choice between a genuine interest in one's own (a real concern to help and protect) and the unwelcome inquisitiveness of strangers whose lack of local community involvement gives them no acknowledged right to be interested.

Physical design cannot take care of all this, but it can encourage the kind of interest on which community cohesion and neighborly self-protection can be based. It is greatly helped by the fact that crime in some of the urban areas is increasingly impersonal; it thrives on the lack of interest of neighbors in each other. If physical design can encourage the kind of self-protective interest that originally inspired people to build walls around their cities, then new subgroups can be built up to make crime more difficult to commit. Undoubtedly, in

[f]The grouping of households or families in a pattern of collective responsibility for each others behavior has been a well-tried system since the feudal days of compurgation. It has been revised by a number of totalitarian regimes in the form of comrade committees; block gauleiters; or street, courtyard, factory, or school committees, the members of which look after each other. This has not only been for crime prevention, (although it has been very effective in controlling crime) it has also been designed for a more positive integration of local groups with development of and loyalty to, national policies—and for greater self-help at a local level.

modern cities crime is much easier as a result of lack of involvement among people. On the one hand, it is far easier for a person to mug a stranger than to attack a relative, neighbor, or friend. Moreover, it is easier to beat someone who no one locally will attempt to protect. On the other hand, it is the complete privacy and isolation of city living that makes this retreat from community self-protection not only possible but seemingly desirable.

The way in which physical planning itself can create crime should not be overlooked. Reference has already been made to the "communityless" housing estates in prewar England from which there was an increasing amount of juvenile delinquency. This resulted partly, at least, because there were so few outlets for youthful enterprise and vigor. And mention is made below of the thin walls and thoughtlessly placed shared amenities that often provoke trouble between neighbors. There are other ways that physical planning can create crime, e.g., inadequate street lighting, weak locks on doors, poor window fastenings, poor layouts, or rooms from which it is difficult to communicate with neighbors. It seems that wherever buildings are designed on the assumption that they will not be broken into, that people can always move in and out of them safely, and that people will not take advantage of physical weaknesses or oversight in design, there is a possibility of crime. This is not to say that crime prevention should be the main consideration in physical design, but rather that it should not be as overlooked as it has been in the past. Obviously total security in design or planning would mean virtual immobility for everyone. No one could possibly afford this. However, a study of the advantages that criminals have taken of building design could lead to better crime prevention. Always, of course, this has to be balanced against costs; just as, in a more general sense, freedom and security have to be balanced in any free society.

Obviously a great many of the extra security devices that city dwellers now have to buy (e.g. double locks, electronic alarms, TV surveillance) can be made regular features of residential buildings. Some voluntary groups, such as the Quakers, have mobilized neighbors in high-risk crime areas to bring immediate help to each other by ringing hand bells or blowing whistles when any one is being attacked. Such mobilization can be simplified if homes are built to make such mobilization easier and the escape of criminals more difficult. Better street lighting, the judicious placing of warning signals, and some of the precautions now taken against fire can be adapted readily for crime prevention. Similarly, banks, business premises, and office blocks can be designed so as to ensure that corridors are overseen by people at work, premises are more easily secured, communications are easier, doors are more readily supervised, and outlets are quickly closed to cut off escape when alarms are sounded. In the centers of cities, roads and streets can be designed to make it easier for regular traffic to make way for fast moving police vehicles. In Canton in China physical design for the protection of streets at night consisted of large doors that could be closed at a certain hour—and these have been used to prevent crime in more modern times. The idea is adaptable to modern circumstances, e.g., electronic barriers could be devised and erected when emergencies arise. Such devices may interfere to some extent with absolute freedom of movement, but some communities might prefer this to untrammelled crime.

The general principle behind physical planning for the crime prevention is to make criminal behavior a high-risk behavior—not only high risk of detection and of observation but high risk of capture and prosecution. Obviously, much more needs to be known about the effects that different kinds of structures have upon behavior. This is time absorbing and experimental, but if physical planners begin now to build the concept of crime prevention into their designs, great progress can be made in the years ahead. By monitoring the crime rates associated with different designs it may be possible to isolate some of the effects of design and physical planning upon behavior.

This is not to suggest, however, that crime necessarily flows from the physical environment. The mere fact that more law abiding persons than offenders come from the same types of structures and neighborhoods casts a great deal of doubt on any such proposition. However, modern cities offer great opportunities for those who learn how to use the impersonality of building types against others. The wealthier residents who require large gardens and high fences to ensure privacy have, by the same token, cut themselves off from neighbors when they are likely to need them most. The concern for living one's own life in the proximity of others in high-rise apartments has made it easy for intruders to pass as residents before or after crimes. The luxuriant gardens cultivated by suburbanites often hide their premises and give cover to intruders. Parks and playing fields have become dangerous simply because they are lonely places after dark, badly lighted, or easy refuge. Even the crowding of students on the campus has made it relatively simple for nonstudents to infiltrate and eventually dominate a scene to which they do not really belong. It is too easy for distant gas stations to be robbed; for perpetrators of crime to merge with busy shopping crowds; for stolen cars to be parked near banks for getaway after the attack; for subway stations to be used for crime because they are thoughtlessly designed, lonely, or not placed near to residents; for windows to be forced or door locks broken; or for vandalism to take place when crowds have dispersed. A more careful study of public habits, public safety needs, and police requirements would lead to the kind of physical planning that would *inter alia* make crime more difficult to commit and much easier to detect and deal with.

Physical Planning and Criminal Justice Services

Corrections. Some years ago an issue of the United Nation's *International Review of Criminal Policy* was devoted to prison architecture. A number of designs and plans were published for the benefit of those designing prisons.

Considerations of safe custody, space in cells, the most effective planning of buildings for easy surveillance, and provisions for training, industry, leisure, and convenient administration were incorporated in the designs. Then, just a few years ago, the United Nations Social Defence Research Institute in Rome mounted a project for correctional institutional architecture, which at the time of this writing is yet unpublished in full.[26] This second initiative was overtaken, however, by the growing dissatisfaction in the U.S. and Europe with prisons of all kinds—on the accumulating evidence that prisons seemed to be failing to either reform criminals or prevent crime.

With the influential demands that there be no further prison building, the interest in prison or institutional design has waned in recent times. Yet, it is clear that when all prisoners who can be safely released to the community or to specialized hostels have been diverted from prisons, there will still be a hard core of dangerous offenders who have to be kept in custody. This will greatly change the requirements for the buildings that will have to be used. Whereas before provision had to be made for a mixed group of compliant offenders, the future regimes for the hard core will have to emphasize safe custody, consistent with full recognition of human rights and the implementation of the United Nations Standard Minimum Rules for the Treatment of Offenders. To date, there has been relatively little thought given to the future needs of the correctional institutions, yet there is great scope for imaginative physical planning for the changing needs of the correctional authorities.

On September 21, 1971, Ada Louise Huxtable published an article in the *New York Times* entitled "New Prison Designs Stress Human Elements." She pointed out that since Attica, changes have come in prison design. Whereas in the earlier buildings the environment had been measured by the requirements of the authorities, it was now to be measured by its effect on men:

The difference between a maximum- and minimum-security prison is defined by the time it takes to cut through a steel bar, or by the height of a wall. The standard design criteria of prison architecture have had little to do with the lives of men. . . .

The design of the new institutions is much more than cosmetic. It does not just add new facades and materials to outmoded concepts. It starts with basic changes in social philosophy and functions in custodial and treatment programs. This radically revises plans and layouts and the kinds of facilities provided and how they are used. It even changes the hardware. It ends with a different type of building.[27]

The author then describes the plans for New York City's Metropolitan Correctional Center—a $12 million building for 400 detainees, most on remand.[28]

Are institutions to be smaller, less open, more electronically equipped, and designed for more individual attention or more varied group sessions? Will there be a requirement for a wide range of small hostels with different degrees of safe custody or community involvement? Will a better-educated and imaginative correctional service call for more scope for experimentation with different facilities for inmate-community liaison? What are the implications for physical design of the need for balance between community protection and the rights and dignities of those to be incarcerated?

Those who could, in the past, be trusted in open institutions can probably be dealt with just as well by a variety of community measures. Does this mean that future prisons will all need to be closed in the more rigid sense of the term, or will there be scope for further subdivision of the dangerous offenders to see to what extent they can be trusted outside the walls? Will such a variety of facilities be better in a single complex, or will there be enough staff to allow for dispersion to different types of accommodation? Physical planning could be very important in the development of a new era in correctional services.

Courts. The courts are changing with perhaps more dependence on modern facilities for recording proceedings. Further, the traditional placements of defense, prosecution, judge, jury, and accused in the court room could well be modified in the years ahead. With extensions of legal aid and a public more aware of their legal rights, it seems inevitable that the number of court rooms per person will increase in the years ahead, offering more scope for physical design, a varied use of space, and rearrangement reflecting modern needs.

Police. The physical designs necessary to meet the changing styles of law enforcement are likely to show more variation in the years ahead. Neighborhood policing, more effective use of modern communications, increasing civilian functions, the move towards greater police-public cooperation, and the computerization of data are all indications that the older-type police station may be re-thought in the future.

The placement of police facilities in both towns and rural districts to achieve law enforcement objectives is likely to be given more consideration. The juxtapositioning of police and courts with remand facilities, the link-up of police buildings with built-in alarms in vulnerable buildings, and the increasing participation of police in youth clubs and community affairs will necessitate attention to physical planning that will help to make the police more effective and more readily available when and where they are needed.

The building of training facilities for the police, incorporating many features that can simulate police working conditions outside, might also provide scope for more ingenuity by architects seeking to translate police needs into practice.

Crime Prevention and Zonal or Regional Planning

While the main concern of this book is sectoral planning, i.e., taking a whole nation as a unit, it is obvious that in many countries the greatest accumulation of planning experience has been in connection with special planning in local zones or regions. In the free enterprise countries particularly, special development areas, new towns, slum clearance, urban renewal, and similar projects have patterned an approach to planning that has been at once more limited and more general than the sectoral national planning already discussed. From the redesigning of city centers through the creation of new (sometimes satellite) towns to the more general development of cities and their regional hinterlands, there has been a vast concern with planning and its implementation and with providing for the physical, economic, and social needs (or anticipated needs) of future inhabitants.

For a long time, in the developing countries, there was a division of opinion between experts as to whether the "take off" to self-sustaining growth could best be achieved by spreading development resources across the country to balance agricultural and industrial growth or by concentrating resources on special growth areas and relying upon these to extend their benefits via a ripple effect across the country. Naturally, political considerations usually made it difficult for any government to neglect some areas for the benefit of others, even in the short run, so the controversy has never been satisfactorily resolved. In the free-enterprise developed countries the interest has been rather different, being concerned more with bringing poor regions up to the level of the more prosperous areas or in deliberately decentralizing urban settlements.

Regional planning is not new of course. Its principles can be traced from the Great Wall of China, through the planning of Greek cities, the road system of the Roman Empire, the design of Renaissance cities, to the canal and railway systems of European countries in more recent times. It has been exemplified by Holland's land reclamation and water control projects at a local level, by the regional development and urban renewal programs in the United States, by the New Towns Development schemes of the United Kingdom, and by the French planning for Paris and the South West. Communist countries have practiced a kind of interregional planning within the context of their more comprehensive national plans, e.g., the electrification of Russia.[29]

The objectives of regional planning in the developed countries have not always been based on economic development alone. Considerations of social equity and, more recently, environmental management have been equally important. While regional planning (outside of communist countries) falls short of the perspectives required for more comprehensive national designing, it involves very much the same principles and is, without doubt, of direct significance to crime prevention in the areas where it takes place. There is often a more direct relationship between a plan and its execution or implementation in regional planning than in national planning—and there can be a more direct local feedback.

Two main factors may be identified as the motivating elements in regional planning in the postwar (and immediate prewar period) in the developed countries. On the one hand, economic growth had usually benefited some areas more than others, and there was a felt need to redress the balance. On the other hand, the increasing concentration of urban settlement had obviously emphasized the need to provide alternative patterns of population distribution.

Because economic factors have not always been paramount in regional planning, the need for the incorporation of social planning requires little emphasis here. It has been recognized in England since the slum clearance of the prewar era demonstrated the problems inherent in ignoring slum lifestyles. The disregard of community interrelationships, which took no account of neighborliness, mutual self-help, or the sense of community in the crowded slums, via the local public houses, corner shops, churches etc., caused such concern that it created a lively awareness, after the war, of the need for relating physical facilities to population needs, pedestrian and traffic safety, and convenience for residents. Special attention was, and is, paid to the needs of children and youth. Judiciously placed shopping centers, community halls, churches, and recreational facilities have characterized town planning in both England and America, with the neighborhood unit concept as the prevailing theme.

Community growth is not entirely a function of physical conditions. Perhaps rather less than sufficient attention has been paid to the ways in which unplanned factors enter into the process of community cohesion—perhaps by the way in which settlements are developed or administered after the planning has been realized in the physical amenities. Similarly, the way in which the design or arrangement of buildings contributes to the quality of social relationships could have attracted more interest than it has to date. The spacing of dwellings is obviously going to affect social intercommunication. So too, building for smaller or larger family units or providing for separate or joint facilities for washing, garbage disposal, or television reception can greatly affect social interaction. Neighborhood quarrels, which occupy the courts and may sometimes even end in crimes such as assault, are not infrequently provoked by the lack of thought accorded the implications of shared facilities. Landings, stair cases, and elevators for which tenants have a joint responsibility can be the cause of disagreements; the placing of drains or water tanks for physical convenience rather than social concern can be a nuisance for some more than others and can lead to problems where tolerance is low. The thickness of walls can mean either problems of privacy or greater communication or surveillance; and a situation in which meters or master switches are accessible to unauthorized persons is a possible problem. All these examples illustrate the effect of physical design on social intercourse—and sometimes *inter alia* on crime prevention.

In 1962 the Royal Institute of British Architects published a study entitled "The Architect and his Office," which demonstrated that in a selected group of sixty architects' offices, the way in which the offices were combined or disposed could affect the devolution of responsibility and the management policies that were adopted. While this could illustrate the way in which physical design helps determine the organization of work, it might also indicate the effect of management policies or the effect of the way available offices were used. The point is, however, that there is an undoubted relationship between social organization and physical arrangement. This is a conclusion that could well be made use of in the development of more effective crime prevention techniques. Of course, crime prevention cannot be the main objective; but the knowledge gained about community groupings, physical factors in the evolution of subcultures, and the need for community participation in correctional service work and the central location of courts and police could well be used to make crime more difficult to commit and easier to detect and discourage.

There will always be an interaction and a feedback between physical, regional, or zonal planning and the social relationship or patterns of social organization. This need not fuel any arguments that social theories are paramount to the forms of planning or that planning is deterministic of behavior. Rather, is it the kind of interaction typical of nature and nurture? Neither one fully determines the other; they are mutually responsive to the contexts and stimuli that each provides for the other. In this connection it is relevant that some of the new towns that have been developed have proved to be more socially viable and more socially integrative than others. Some plans have taken their shape, in part at least, from the social, economic, or political interests involved in the evolution of the plan. In some cases, the people to be served have participated at each stage of plan formulation; while in other cases, they have remained very much on the periphery. The full consequences of all this have not been sufficiently monitored, and it is significant that criminologists have evidenced little interest in the criminological implications of different forms of regional planning. Nor have they yet sought to trace the possible connections between crime rates and the different styles of regional planning and different types of implementation.

The process of regional planning may be divided into five steps:

1. The data gathering stage—when all available information about the region and its present and projected inhabitants is compiled
2. The formulation of the plan, with integration of all sectors to meet plan objectives
3. Programming—subdivision of the plan into programs and projects
4. Implementation—often in timed phases
5. Evaluation—usually at fixed time intervals

Most regional planners are ready to accept the need for sociologists or social workers to survey the population before planning is undertaken. They are, by now, also well accustomed to this type of data gathering before delving into the economic, social, environmental, and physical developments they may have in mind. A number of writers (notably Patrick Geddes and the writers for the

British Institute of Community Studies, the American Institute of Planners, and the Regional Science Association) have underlined the need for preliminary surveys before planning. The importance of such advance studies is emphasized by the innumerable examples of regional planning frustrated because of inadequate social surveys at preliminary stages. This writer had the experience of evaluating an Iranian industrial project for which there had been innumerable feasibility studies in determining site, economic prospects, and investment required; but there had been no survey at all of the type and quality of unemployment in the area the project was designed to serve. As a result, to be viable it had to import skilled labor from other areas, leaving the local unskilled inhabitants without the extra employment opportunities they needed.

Usually, there are no preliminary surveys of the crime rates or crime potentials. Criminal justice services have rarely been brought into planning—and even if they had, it is doubtful that they would have had the survey information necessary to make useful suggestions. This, then, is a gap in planning at the regional level, which it would be relatively simple to remedy.

However, surveys before planning by no means exhaust the contribution to regional planning that sociologists, social workers, and crime prevention planners can make. In the more general sense of social planning, there are a number of questionable assumptions underlying the restriction of social input to preliminary surveys. Since these are both fact and attitude gathering surveys, it should be noted that the facts may be outdated almost as fast as they are collected and people do not always know what they really require to satisfy their own wants or needs. Often people surveyed are not in sufficient possession of the facts necessary to make choices. Frequently, present needs may be quite far removed from future necessities, simply because it is never easy to forecast future incomes and resources.

This is one kind of complication, but there are others. For instance, sociological inquiries of the kind that have been carried out so far have been typically treated as handmaidens to physical design and the planning of investments and developments. Clearly, formulation of the plan when the data have been supplied will also depend upon certain social principles and values that need to be made more explicit in the planning process. Programming and implementation will also be affected by social imperatives and attitudes. Evaluation according to objectives realized also cannot be entirely divorced from social factors. In the same general context, there is a need to consider the criminogenic aspects of plan formulation and implementation. In evaluation too, it is clear that standards of public safety and freedom from crime have to be taken into account.

It is probably a mistake to regard social inputs as subordinate to general planning or to subordinate the planning process to purely social or social-problem imperatives. Rather, both should be taken in the broader perspective of the future society. Not only should possible preferences be examined but also attitudes and expectations, class, group, and occupational patterns, and economic and social objectives. This is easier where regional planning has become a part of more general national planning, but there have been moves to use regional planning as an *approach* to national planning.[30]

More recently in the concept of *total architecture* and Doxiadis' ambitious approach to *ekistics* as a science of human settlement, there have been indications of a widening of regional or physical planning schemes to incorporate all aspects of human habitation—except crime.[g] Once again, the underlying illusion is that all people are naturally not criminals, immune from criminal exploitation, and always likely to react positively to national planning.

Perhaps nowhere in the world has there been such a direct link between criminologists and regional planners as that which is now embryonic in Australia. The Australian Institute of Criminology has been invited to work directly with the Albury-Wodonga Development Corporation in plans for a new growth center between Melbourne and Sydney. Also, the Sydney City Council has expressed a wish to use persons trained by the Institute to assist in the redevelopment of the city center, where courses for crime prevention planners (from the economic and planning services as well as the criminal justice services) are now being conducted annually by the Institute.

Regional planners have a great opportunity to pioneer a new phase of crime prevention planning. They can cut across sectoral boundaries, integrate social and economic development, and thereby evolve programs capable of dealing effectively with local social problems—including crime. To do this, however, regional planners need to add a crime prevention dimension to their plan organization and bring crime prevention considerations into their data gathering, plan formulation, programming, and implementation processes. They will also be required to take crime levels into account in evaluation of the results of regional or zonal planning.

Notes

1. Martin Mayer, *The Bankers*, Weybright and Tolley, 1974.

2. See David Owen, "The Great Computer Robbery," in *The Listener*, 2 October 1975, p. 434, based on a radio documentary written by David Owen and presented by Paul Vaughan.

3. W.W. Rostow, *The Stages of Economic Growth* (Cambridge: Cambridge University Press, 1960).

4. R.F. Harrod and E.D. Domar, *Essays on the Theory of Economic Growth* (New York: Oxford University Press, 1957).

5. Robert Gilpin, *American Science and Nuclear Weapons Policy* (Princeton: Princeton University Press, 1962), p. 30.

[g]Since this was written Doxiade's classifications have been excluded to include crime prevention.

6. A. Waterston, *Development Planning: Lessons of Experience* (Baltimore: Johns Hopkins University Press, 1965), p. 26. © The Johns Hopkins University Press, 1965.

7. "Framework for an Analysis of Decision-making in the Social Sectors," paper prepared by the United Nations Research Institute for Social Development, Geneva, p. 1.

8. Herbert J. Gans, "Social Planning and Urban Planning," in *International Encyclopedia of Social Sciences* 11/12, ed. David L. Sills (New York: The Macmillan Company and the Free Press, 1968).

9. J. Tinbergen, "Economic Planning: Western Europe," ibid., p. 103.

10. Naomi Caiden and Aaron Wildavsky, *Planning and Budgeting in Poor Countries* (New York: John Wiley and Sons, 19   ), p. 264ff.

11. Ibid.

12. W. Clifford, *Introduction to African Criminology* (Nairobi: Oxford University Press, 1974), p. 23, and note 8 on p. 92.

13. Ann Stafford, *The Age of Consent* (London: Hodder and Stoughton, 1964), p. 29.

14. See Edgar Salin and Rene L. Frey, "Friedrich List," in *International Encyclopedia of Social Sciences* 9/10, op. cit., pp. 409-412.

15. Edward H. Carr, *History of Soviet Russia*, vols. 5-7 (New York: The Macmillan Company, 1958-1964).

16. Ferdinand Zweig, *The Planning of Free Societies* (London: Secker and Warburg, 1942).

17. J. Tinbergen, op. cit.

18. E. Lederer, "National Economic Planning," in *Encyclopedia of Social Services* 11 (New York: The Macmillan Company, 1933), pp. 197-205.

19. See, for example Ezra F. Vogel, *Canton under Communism* (Cambridge, Mass.: Harvard University Press, 1969), p. 272.

20. See relationships between *armatoloi* and *klephts* in mountainous areas of the Ottoman Empire in Richard Clogg, *The Struggle for Greek Independence* (New York: Archon Books, 1973), p. 8.

21. U.S. 93d Cong., 3d Sess., Senate Select Committee on Small Business, *1973 Hearing on Impact of Crime on Small Business*, part 2, appendix, "Criminal Redistribution Systems and their Economic Impact on Small Businesses," Washington, D.C., 1973, p. 270.

22. See "A Reporter at Large," *The New Yorker*, December 9, 1974.

23. Patrick G. Ryan, *Can White-Collar Crime Affect the Economy?* (Toronto: Carleton University Press, 1972).

24. J.F. Mortlock, *Experience of a Convict Transported for Twenty-one Years*, eds. G.A. Wilkes and A.G. Mitchell (Sydney: Sydney University Press, 1966).

25. Oscar Newman, *Defensible Space: Crime Prevention through Urban Design* (New York: The Macmillan Company, 1972).

26. To be issued soon, *Prison Architecture*, United Nations Social Defence Research Institute (London: Architectural Press Ltd., 1976).

27. Ada Louise Huxtable, "New Prison Designs Stress Human Elements," in *The New York Times*, September 21, 1971. © 1971 by the New York Times Company. Reprinted with permission.

28. See also Wolf von Eckardt, "New Design Helps Point the Way to Prison Reform," in *The Washington Post*, October 7, 1971.

29. A. Kulinski, "Macro Regional Planning in the Developed Countries," UNRISD/71/C.32, United Nations Research Institute for Social Development, Geneva, March 1971.

30. See *Regional Factors in National Planning*, Natural Resources Committee (Washington, D.C.: U.S. Government Printing Office, 1935); also M.D. Rivkin, *Area Development for National Growth: The Turkish Experience* (New York: Praeger, 1965); and Walter Stohr, *Regional Planning as a Necessary Tool for the Comprehensive Development of a Country*, U.N. Symposium, Warsaw, Poland, 14-28 June 1971.

2 National and Social Planning: Interrelationships with Crime Prevention

National Planning

Any national plan is a reflection of a country's determination to run its own affairs for the benefit of its citizens. It is a government commitment to development and will usually specify its aims and objectives as well as the means adopted to achieve those goals. It is an attempt to improve upon the former tendencies of many governments to make decisions in response to pressures brought to bear on them by political forces within their own frontiers (or from outside). The national plan seeks to provide a countrywide overview of public investments and expenditures not only to meet immediate requirements but to look ahead several years and guide the economy into desired channels. Planning seeks better and more logical approaches to the appropriations and allocations of national resources than the inclination of authorities simply to respond to local crises and the influences of the moment. It goes far beyond the early practice of governments to live by their budgets from year to year. It involves projections or predictions of future trends or problems, the collection of data on available resources with a view to mobilizing them for specific purposes, an explicit and conscious awareness of the bases upon which decisions are made, the adoption of clear aims or intentions and their disclosure, the formulation of broad strategies to ensure that the aims are achieved, and the selection of the methods or techniques most likely to achieve the ends desired.

Caiden and Wildavsky have argued very convincingly that this is an ambitious approach to human and national affairs, which cannot really be achieved. They suggest that it demands too much knowledge, power, and resources, and they prefer a less unrealistic use of a budgetary procedure.[1]

We have already criticized the way in which planners may be inclined by the nature of their task to act like God or assume that rationality will solve everything. This is very far from abandoning the planning concept or depending entirely on budgetary procedures. Planners have been conceited in the past, have often built in protective devices that would excuse their failures, or have refused to face the real irrationality or cultural complexity of the societies to which they sought to apply their models. But, as has been well said, there is nothing so practical as a good theory; and even if planning has been too idealistic or too far removed from reality, its value for a world increasingly conscious of its past mistakes should not be underestimated.

Planning may be from above by specialists (or politicians with specialist

49

advice) deciding what would be best for the country—as was the case when Japan was entirely reorganized on Western lines at the time of the Meiji Restoration or when Turkey shook off its past under Kemal Ataturk. Or planning can come from below: each area drawing up its own plan for incorporation into a nationally coordinated scheme. It may be a combination of interests from above and below, with or without adequate public consultation and discussion before each step is formulated into the final draft. Iran's Plan Organization in the middle 1960s had both the resources and authority to implement its own plans, circumventing if necessary the usual Ministries. Later the Ministries reassumed authority with the incorporation of Plan Organization experts and officials into their Ministerial establishments. Before the independence of the colonies many of the colonial powers provided for decentralized planning, but the real decision-makers were the local officials of the governmental departments and public discussion tended to be limited. Political considerations inevitably intervene when it seems that too much power may be flowing to a planning body. Thus the Philippine National Economic Council gradually lost its control, and the 4-year plan of 1971 was prepared by the President's economic staff.[2]

In some of the free enterprise countries there is very little in the way of centralized national planning, if one excludes advisory councils and the central control of reserve banks or currency issues. The emphasis is rather on local, provincial, or state plans, on the regional or zonal planning of cities and their immediate hinterlands, or on the development of special new growth centers, as in Australia.

One must recognize here, however, the degree of central government oversight of local or regional planning implied by the United Kingdom's 1934 Special Area Act, which acknowledged the central government's responsibility for managing industrial location and regional development to deal with concentrations of unemployment; by the National Resources Planning Board set up by the U.S. in the prewar years to commission regional development plans; by the steady extension of French government control of provincial planning; and by the national agency set up by the Dutch in 1941 to coordinate subnational planning. These were often limited in practice by constitutional or political constraints on full control, but they show a greater degree of national interest in local schemes and the machinery for making resources available locally for nationally approved projects. The form of national planning is therefore varied because of political, cultural, constitutional, or geographical factors.

Even within the communist states (or centrally planned economies) there are variations. Yugoslavia, for example, has had a great deal more decentralization in its planning than has been typical of Eastern European countries with their:

. . . complex apparatus of government and party officials similar in most respects to that prevailing in the U.S.S.R.[3]

In 1953 and 1954, Czechoslovakia and Poland, respectively, replaced the earlier procedures of central allocations of resources to state enterprises on the basis of a coordination of the estimates from the enterprises themselves (planning from below) with a system of reliance on ministries (planning from above), which greatly reduced the planning bureaucracy and administrative costs.[4] And China rapidly became disenchanted with the Soviet pattern of centralized planning and opted for a greater degree of spontaneity and regional autonomy.

A plan will be based upon projections of investment, savings, income, consumption, rates of return, levels of demand and prospects of supply, imports and exports, manpower, levels of skills, health, education, and employment prospects. Indicative planning also means the erecting of signposts for private sectors, in particular, to follow. The expected rise in Gross National Product and the distribution of this increase through the various sectors (health, education, forestry, commerce, and industry) gives a useful guide for those in private industry and commerce who are seeking to assess market demand, or the availability of money to spend. And this is particularly so where the indication is of the level of the government's own investment in the various enterprises, since this shows where the funds will flow and where demand will be increased and incomes will be more readily available for consumer expenditure.

It is far easier to discuss the broad principles of planning than it is to specify the details, because, as already shown, the interpretation and implementation of planning principles differs widely at the different levels of application. The same terms can mean different things depending upon whether one is dealing with public or private sectors; local, regional, or national planning; or with policies or programs. Moreover, planning grew out of practice. In the postcolonial countries it often emerged from the postwar provisions of funds by the metropolitan countries for local development. These extra funds were separated from the budgets for ongoing services to avoid their becoming no more than supports of the regular budget. The idea was to prevent the disappearance of the extra funds into routine ministerial demands for "more of the same" and also to encourage the development of new (and especially visible) projects like roads, schools, communications, etc. Typically, there would be a regular budget each year and, alongside this, a development budget extending over 5 or more years, intended mainly for capital investment. Incidentally, it is interesting to observe that these separate development funds in the colonies often provided for new police stations, police cars, and communications. Since the preindependence years were also, quite frequently, years of political confrontation, demonstrations, strikes and riots, it seemed logical to provide for improvements in police services to provide for basic law and order. Israel therefore has its Taggart police stations built for a seige, which grew out of this history, and many African countries inherited fine networks of police installations.

In passing, it should be noted that the distinction that is still not infrequently made between development expenditures, mainly on capital investment, and the recurrent budget is often largely artificial. The difference frequently disappears in practice when large amounts spent on equipment or maintenance in recurrent budgets can amount to a substantial capital investment—or when the minor items in a capital budget seem to overlap the items normally found in a recurrent budget. This is a habitual approach to immediate and longer-term expenditures, which probably has greater psychological than rational justification.[5]

In other countries—especially in Western Europe—the recourse to planning came from wartime mobilizations of resources and distribution systems to ration allocations according to priorities. Here again, the one-year budgeting was not appropriate, and separate control systems had to be devised covering several years. In the communist countries planning flowed from the public ownership of the means of production and the need to determine needs and requirements that earlier had been responsive to market price mechanisms or capitalistic monopolies. Lately, in the United States, where national planning was more difficult because of the fifty separate states, the planning procedures have grown out of the need to tie annual budgets to longer-term objectives and to avoid *ad hoc* and unreliable programs. Since the Viet Nam War period, the United States has made an effort to incorporate the yearly budgeting into three-year programs. This is known as *program budgeting* and is described below. Thus, in several areas there has been a transition from yearly estimates for ongoing services (with separate provisions for anything in the nature of capital investment or longer-term developments) to broader approaches absorbing the annual budgets into more comprehensive schemes and becoming in the process more national and wide-ranging than before.[a]

Taking planning in its widest national sense, as practiced by the centrally planned economies and the developing countries generally, it is clear from actual practice that a national plan is intended to serve a number of functions. It is often expected to:

1. Symbolize the determination of a country to promote development.
2. Arouse enthusiasm for development—thus making it easier to mobilize support.
3. Coordinate the activities of government departments.
4. Be an attempt to anticipate the total impact of alternative courses of action on the different elements of the national economy.
5. Provide the private sector with a basis for expectations.
6. Be an aid to, or a substitute for, the market mechanism as an instrument of resource allocation. (Indeed it is the alleged inability of the market mechanism to create socially desirable patterns of resource allocation that accounts for public sectors and for the planning approach.)

The policy of a country will determine its planning objectives and they may

_____
[a]See section below on program budgeting.

not always coincide. Developing countries, for example, may have to choose from a combination of:

1. Augmenting the inadequate levels of public consumption
2. Accelerating growth by further investment in the means of production
3. Creating more employment
4. Improving foreign exchange reserves

Currently, the more advanced countries are faced with the dilemma of maintaining high levels of employment and consumption amidst galloping inflation; and these problems are not as remote from the issue of crime as they at first seem. They are attributable to an expansionary boom creating shortages in key materials, huge balances of speculative and stateless funds resulting from high interest rates, the windfalls of currency revaluations (which impoverish millions), and energy deficiencies not unrelated to a squeeze by producers for political ends), and (to no small extent) a long-term neglect of widespread international operations by illegal syndicates and multinational companies that circumvent local laws. The effects on living standards are seeping down to the "fourth world," developing countries that never had much room for economic maneuver, anyway, and are now faced with more expensive essential imports at a time when they can least afford them. Planning at the national level is more difficult in modern times, therefore, than in the earlier period of confidence in monetary values, sources of supply, and employment levels. The policies likely to be most efficient and productive are not so readily available as they were once thought to be; the older principles and the established models no longer apply. Nevertheless, plans will be made according to the policies thought to be the most efficacious by the governments concerned. And it is evident that national planning will be very similar in its procedures to the pattern outlined above.

Mobilizing Support

The Five Year Plan for Ceylon 1972-1976 is introduced by a foreword from the Prime Minister, which points out that although the country has fertile soil, abundant natural resources, and an educated population, it depends on other countries for food and essential requirements. There is a serious problem of unemployment, a large national debt, and a shortage of foreign exchange. The Prime Minister points out that the Five Year Plan is designed to address these problems and that it is the failure to understand the nature of the problem and the failure to plan the organization of resources according to a set of clearly defined objectives that have left the country in such a helpless situation. Then the Prime Minister says:

In placing the Plan before the people I call upon my fellow countrymen to rally around its program and policies and salvage the country from its present plight. The building of a socialist democracy required the unremitting effort of the entire nation. The Five Year Plan shows a way out, but it involves patriotism, sacrifice, hard work, and devotion to duty from every one of us.

Here is the call to arouse the people to the effort needed to achieve the objectives.

Zaire, Zambia, and a number of other African countries have used their plans to implement a national drive for the kind of economic independence thought to be necessary to match their political independence. Tanzania, in particular, has its plan as part of a reorientation of social, economic, and political life, more in keeping with African communal and traditional values.

In a similar vein, Papua New Guinea, which achieved independence as this was being written, introduced its Strategies for Nationhood with eight specific aims, namely:

1. To increase the proportion of the economy under local control.
2. To equalize the distribution of economic benefits.
3. To decentralize economic growth, planning, and government spending.
4. To concentrate on small-scale business development.
5. To reduce imports and encourage self reliance.
6. To improve the ratio of government spending from locally raised revenues.
7. To advance women.
8. To extend government control of those sectors of the economy where this is necessary.

These are aims as notably political and social as they are economic, and they are designed to attract wide public support for the planning.

The Ideals and Motivation

While primarily economic and social, a plan cannot avoid certain political overtones, which therefore it would be unrealistic to ignore.[b] These percolate down to affect the agencies involved. The idealism of a plan can both make or break it. If soundly based, the call to action that a plan proposes may motivate the effort needed to carry it over innumerable difficulties. If ill conceived or too obviously unrealistic, the necessary efforts may not be made or may lack the conviction necessary for success. If class, caste, ethnic, or sectional interests of any kind are unfairly served, or if the bulk of the population is not made to feel that it has a legitimate and recognized share in the benefits as well as the

[b]Indeed in some of the foregoing examples political objectives are conscious and are made paramount.

burdens, then the plan is hampered, if not doomed, from the beginning. Social justice and equity can be as important as purely economic or social factors if a truly national effort is being sought. Besides its political aspects, then, it may be acknowledged that there is a social-psychological element to a plan, which it would be equally unwise to underestimate. Not infrequently, it is such psychological, social, or political considerations that determine the choice of alternatives between most efficient and less efficient approaches to national development problems. Sometimes it is for purely psychological or political reasons that a less efficient program may be considered as being the more effective for a plan.

In terms of crime prevention the ideal that motivates the implementation of a plan can be very valuable. It can reduce conflicts and promote toleration. Working together for a common purpose unites people, breaks down barriers, and reduces many of the subcultural divisions, which have been shown to justify, if not actually to promote, fierce disagreements, conflict, and some kinds of crime. It may be said that an inspiring and unifying plan is, therefore, itself crime preventative.

Coordination and Direction

In the process of allocating resources to achieve its goals, a plan seeks to coordinate public and private efforts at the national and provincial levels. It aims at coordinating the work of government ministries but also, as we have seen, at providing the private sector with a clear outline of governmental intentions so that it can plan its own future.

However, coordination, though central to any effective planning, is one of the most difficult areas of resource mobilization and allocation. Some plans are no more than compromise solutions to long periods of bargaining by the ministries or agencies for the available resources. This may not be very rational, but it is a fact of life. And here again, it would be unwise to discount the interplay of political and social interests in determining the shape of a plan. Some countries have made little headway because the planning ministry or organization was not sufficiently powerful to resolve existing conflicts of local or national interests.

In Chile, for instance, the *Oficina de Planification National* (ODEPLAN) was a professional and technical planning unit that fed with specialist help and data the powerful *Comite Economica*, which was responsible for national economic policy and had the President as its head. Its membership also included the Minister of Finance, the heads of the central and state banks, and representatives of ODEPLAN itself. It had only one voice, therefore, in a council within which the struggle for influence and power was very marked.[6]

One important function of a plan is, therefore, to provide a set of objectives that all the ministries or agencies, central and local, can accept and within which they can subordinate their own vested interests for the common good. Only in this way will coordination of effort become possible. High status central planning councils or committees that determine objectives have been adopted by a number of countries, and this certainly helps. But much depends upon the respective status and power of the ministries and agencies concerned—and upon their willingness to place the plan objective above any sectional ambitions. There are internal politics in planning and inherent bureaucratic restraints that call for as much diplomacy and managerial skills as experience and expertise in planning itself. These have frequently defeated the aims of planning. Indeed, there have been examples of crime, in the form of corruption, infiltrating these higher councils and thus undermining the planning process *ab initio*.

If the guidelines are not sufficiently clear or if they are not too closely adhered to at each district, province, or level, then a nationwide collection of plans prepared from below could well become no more than an exercise in compromise between the varied vested interests and the political groups. In this case, therefore, the plan would be a questionable addition to what is already the ordinary direction of local and central administration. Under the heading of planning, the ministries, agencies, or local councils would be doing much the same as they would have done without any plan. One often sees this where a government offers funds for new locally prepared plans. To obtain the additional funds the older budget applications are dressed up to look like a new plan. But any careful scrutiny will show that there is really no new departure from the older approaches, even though the language of planning is being used. They are just a demand for "more of the same."[c]

In other countries, the central planners, while not going down to such a geographically local level for contributions to the plan, still try to reach down to the future implementers by means of sectoral committees on which the interests of all the different grades of administration are represented. Conceptually this might be regarded as "vertical" participation in the planning process. The various interests are arranged professionally and influence the final plan by means of their national representatives on a variety of national committees—as distinct from the broader district or provincial planning described above, which can be regarded conceptually as "horizontal" participation. This vertical system provides the Planning Ministry or the National Plan Organization with a series of

[c]William Gorham has suggested that planning in the United States is often a rather esoteric activity. Planners are viewed as people who look down the dimly lit road of the future and make predictions or projections of things to come. They are not thought to be intimately concerned with the decisions of today. He writes, "The U.S. Government has never had a Planning Agency of 'a plan'. Some individual agencies have had planning offices but most of them suffered one of two fates; either they planned and nobody listened (the plans here not translated into decisions) or they did not plan (they worked on current problems instead)." From "Sharpening the Knife that Cuts the Public Pie," *Congressional Record*, 5 December 1967, pp. 17861-6.

specialist committees that are both representative and technically equipped to guide the planning once the broad direction has been given by the higher levels of government. Sometimes, of course, a national plan may be compiled by a combination of both "horizontal" and "vertical" participation. This is obviously as desirable as it is more complicated; but it can ensure, if it is done properly, a more comprehensive type of participation in national planning.

The Procedures

The kind of planning that we call national planning is, in effect, an extension of the ordinary budgeting procedures of most governments. The regular appropriations each year for the various departments, agencies, or ministries are reconceived by the planners in terms of the different sectors of the economy, e.g., agriculture, industry, transport, roads, communications, education, health, labor, and social welfare. Then, for planning purposes, a period of four or five years is taken and actual financing or resource allocations are compared to the pattern of the economy as desired by those framing the plan objectives. The existing plant, available or potential resources, income, investment, and expenditure that will be necessary over this period to achieve the declared targets of the plan are projected and proportioned in accordance with the main aims of the plan, e.g., to industrialize or develop the rural economy (or both). The priorities are set, and the broad proportions of available resources to be allocated to the sectors are then determined—usually with built-in provisions for review, reappraisal, or evaluation at predetermined stages of plan implementation.

In addition, however, a total plan prepared in an economy that has private sectors will also have targets for private enterprise. A plan will typically provide for governmental measures to encourage the private decision-makers to fall in line with governmental guidance. Licenses, loans, currency issues, and/or restrictions, taxation, trading permits, and credit controls are various ways in which the government can make its influence felt in the private sectors of the economy. But the extent to which private firms, companies, or interests actually follow the government line will generally be a function of the amount of power that the government is able to exercise in the implementation of its national plan. According to its structure or circumstances, a government is usually able to increase official pressure if it finds that the private sector is not cooperating voluntarily; then, tighter controls or more attractive incentives might be introduced. In some extreme cases, commodities were controlled or rationed, savings deducted from pay or profits, and, in one African country with a serious unemployment problem, all private firms were required to employ 5 percent more labor than they had before. The conditions will differ according to the type of government and the extent of its power over the means of production, and it will naturally be shaped according to the political climate. In any event, it is clear that a government with a plan will need to have at its disposal all the measures necessary to make it work, not only within the official government services but also in those operating outside the government's direct authority. Often the private sector depends so much on the direction that a government is taking (i.e., it depends on government intentions for its contracts, profits, interests, credit, etc.), that it is generally sufficient for the government's own policy and direction to be made known for the private firms to fall into line—even if there may be differences in matters of detail.

After all the consultations, discussions, data gathering, drafts of sectoral plans by ministries or local authorities, and negotiations on contentious or conflicting interests, a national plan is finally drawn up. It will be approved at the national level, but there is always a very lively appreciation that it requires (both for its validity as a feasible plan and for its support by local authorities and the people they serve) a wide measure of participation by the ministries, the provincial or city governments, the various private interests, and the people themselves. As already indicated, some plans are actually formulated from below—each district making its own plan according to broad guidelines laid down by the central planning authority—and submitted to the provincial level where it is considered in combination with all the plans from the other districts in the province and adjusted to fit the total provincial plan. The provinces then forward their plans to the central planning authority, which coordinates these and draws up the final national plan. In the process it is obvious that, at each level, there will be a paring of the schemes submitted. Many proposals will have to be omitted, revised, reformulated, adjusted, modified, or reshaped entirely to fit in with the final plan for the district or province. But, if all those planning at the different levels are able to operate on common guidelines, it is possible for this amalgamation of schemes to result in a national plan of optimal meaning and maximum relevancy for all interests at all levels and in all the different parts of the country. Obviously not everyone will be satisfied. Priority setting alone leaves some better endowed with resources and possible rewards than others; but the aim will naturally be to minimize dissatisfaction—except perhaps where a national emergency or national political imperatives (e.g., as may occur as a result of war or after revolutions) force the sharing of undesirable burdens.

Complications to this broad outline of the planning procedure are introduced when federal governments are considered. There may be separate state plans, but as a rule the federal government also has an overall plan or strategy, which it implements via its own federal agencies. A commonly used technique is that of placing funds at the disposal of the state governments for schemes that they are then invited to submit for approval. In at least one federal state, some of these funds are made contingent upon the submission of local plans for approval, i.e., the states are obliged to plan in order to obtain the funds they will need from federal sources.

National planning obviously depends on government leadership, and in the past its presence or absence has turned largely upon a nation's view of the importance of government control and interference. Capitalism, which traditionally supported private freedom of action, which depended upon the market mechanism, and which has sought to reduce government interference to a minimum has always been an uncongenial setting for comprehensive planning— any kind of government direction reduced the area of free action for the private sector. Socialism, which called for public ownership of the means of production, was committed by definition to widespread government interference and direction. Perhaps neither of these extreme situations or conditions are to be found today in any pure form. As we have seen, under capitalism, absolute freedom of action led to a variety of monopolistic practices, retail price maintenance, and economically powerful financial or business groups trying to dictate wages and prices and thus control all the markets. So in practice, the governments of free enterprise countries have had to intervene in the interests of the society. Conversely, the total controls of authoritarian societies have frequently had to be modified over time to provide for more freedom of choice and wider extensions of privilege. Moreover, a third area of national planning for developing countries highlights the need for concentration on the construction of essential infrastructures and institutions (like roads, airports, technical education, and good public administration), and these depend upon a wide measure of government intervention and outside aid.

But even if pure examples are difficult to find, it is still true that local ideas on the extent to which a government could or should intervene in the economic and social affairs of the nation will still largely determine the role that national planning can play. More particularly, it will serve to determine the shape and scope of the national plan; and effective implementation will always depend upon the way in which the government uses its powers.

The Sectoral Planning

Within the broader context of any national plan, each sector of the economy will have its own subplan. This subplan, like the broader plan, will project resources, set targets, and indicate priorities and allocations. For example, the subplan for the educational sector will show the schools presently existing, their staff and equipment, their annual potential, and their shortcomings. The target for education will have been given in the total plan, and the subplan for the education sector will adopt this and show how the target is to be reached with available resources plus the additional allocations proposed for the next 4 or 5 years, as the case may be. Similarly, in agriculture, the needs of the people for crops to consume, export, and store will be shown, the resources of the farmers and their organizations (e.g., cooperatives and credit societies) will be detailed, and the task ahead defined—as this is measured by the targets and indicated by the shortfalls. The subplan will show the allocations to be made from national resources and the programs or projects to be financed by them.

Zonal or Regional Planning

This has already been dealt with at some length above. Regional planning occurs as a special kind of area planning within the context of a national plan and takes the region rather than the sector as a planning unit—or it has occurred as a kind of concentrated planning where full national planning has not arrived.

Examples. Thailand in its Third Development Plan running from 1971 to 1976 stated that it would aim at:

1. The acceleration of the production of good services—especially for export.
2. The development of education, human resources, and technology.
3. The better utilization of existing construction facilities.
4. Regional, urban, and community development.
5. Investment in support of economic preparedness.

The government therefore provided for a total development expenditure of 100,275 million baht. Of this total, which includes foreign loans and grants as well as self-financing from state enterprises, the economic sector received 43,395 million baht. This comprised 19,475 million baht devoted to communications and transport, 13,695 million baht for agriculture and irrigation, 7,875 million baht for power installations, and 1,480 million baht allocated to industry and mining; commerce and services were to receive 870 million baht. The social sector by comparison was to be given more than 50 percent of the total development budget. Here 56,880 million baht was made available, the lion's share of this going to education, which was given 32,910 million baht. Urban and rural development was allocated 15,080 million baht, health was allocated 6,340 million, and social development was given 2,550 million baht. No doubt the division into economic and social sectors incorporated some overlap; the urban and rural development headings doubtless included provision for improvements that could be regarded as economic, and the economic sector has included some services that might be regarded as social (see "agricultural extension" below). Nevertheless, the attempt of the Thai government to stress its social sector, and especially education, comes out very clearly. Similarly, the priority given to infrastructure is indicated by the fact that the largest share of the money for the economic sector went to this subsector. It should be added, however, that the largest proportion of foreign loans (nearly 5,000 million baht) was made available for communications and transport.

If one examines this distribution of financial resources, one can see that the objectives of the plan are reflected. Therefore, objectives were drawn up for each sector. For example, in agriculture and irrigation the intention was to achieve a 5.1 percent rate of growth per annum as opposed to 4.2 percent in the second plan. To achieve this the specific targets were:

1. To accelerate production, improve quality, and increase exports, promoting *inter alia* the development of agroindustry to raise the income of farmers.
2. To develop crops and livestock in suitably defined zones for agricultural extension, which have definite markets.
3. To improve agricultural extension methods so that agricultural techniques and technical information could more efficiently reach the farmers.
4. To improve natural resources for agricultural production, e.g., water resources, soil fertility, and forestry conservation.
5. To improve agricultural research and find solutions for agricultural problems.
6. To strengthen agricultural institutions with a view to achieving cooperation among farmers in production and marketing, etc.
7. To accelerate existing irrigation development projects.
8. To extend government services to the farmers, especially credit and extension services, and promote greater cooperation and self-help among the farmers.
9. To improve coordination in marketing, so that producers can sell their products at good and stable prices.

Then under each of these objectives, programs and projects were designed to attain the desired effects. For instance, under target 6, above, it was indicated that Thailand now has 991 cooperatives of all farmers with 269,704 families as members, 4,196 farmers groups, 210 people's irrigation associations, and 96 water users associations, the total membership of all these being 695,699 families, i.e., only 14 percent of the 5 million families in agriculture. Therefore, these agricultural institutions are rather weak. The programs and projects for the plan period were designed therefore to establish large multipurpose cooperatives to help farmers in their production and marketing. The strategy was to accelerate the expansion of the irrigation system in the Ministry of National Development's Coordinated Irrigation Projects' area, to transform the present credit cooperatives into large-scale agrobusiness cooperatives, and to promote settlement cooperatives, land rent and land hire purchase cooperatives, and a league of cooperatives. In the third plan, the policy was to combine the various agricultural institutions (except cooperatives) into farmer groups with legal status and the authority they would need to conduct business. These farmers groups were to be formed at the *amphoe* level, so that they might be transformed later into cooperatives.

Similarly, for the power subsector, it was explained in the plan that during the two previous plans the aim had been to build large-scale, high-efficiency electric power plants with low production costs and to erect transmission and distribution lines to connect the various *changwats* and *amphoes*. For the third plan the subsectoral aim was to expand the power generating capacity and sales system, and to gradually lower the power rates so as to improve the well-being of the people and promote various development activities. In addition, rural electrification programs were to be carried out with definite work plans. The specific targets were detailed as:

1. To expand electric power production to meet the national demand, which was expected to increase at a rate of 16.2 percent per annum. Therefore, electric power was to be increased from the present 1,169 megawatts to 2,469 megawatts by 1976.
2. To provide for the rise in sales from 3,000 million kilowatt hours in 1971 to 6,000 million kilowatt hours in 1976, i.e., at a rate of 16.4 percent per annum.
3. To reduce electric power rates. It was expected that even if the national demand for electric power increased at no more than 15.5 percent (i.e., lower than the rate projected above) and if the purchase rate of power from the Nam Ngum dam in Laos was not higher than that produced from internal steam power plants, the Electric Generating Authority of Thailand would be in a position to lower the electric power rates to the sales authorities.

Again, under each of these targets there were more detailed programs and projects to produce the desired results.

To take a second country of the Asian region, Ceylon, in its Five Year Plan 1971-1976, listed its social and economic objectives as follows:

1. To carry through the structural changes in the economy necessary for long-term growth, i.e., by investment in basic industries that can provide the inputs for other industries, the growth of new types of crops, and the creation of entirely new sectors in industry and agriculture based on nontraditional commodities.
2. To implement the short-term measures necessary to correct the growing imbalances in the economy—in particular, the widening gap in the balance of payments and the increasing numbers of the unemployed.
3. To reduce social tensions by the elimination of wasteful consumption and by redistributive measures.
4. To raise the living standards of the low income groups by improving housing and sanitary facilities, raising nutrition levels by increasing the production of essential foods, and gearing the production of consumer goods to the needs of the masses.
5. To take measures to regenerate rural society and make it more attractive to

the young by modernizing agriculture and siting agrobased industries in rural areas.

The plan proposed a total investment of 14,820 million rupees to be divided into 7,040 million rupees for the public sector and 7,780 million rupees for the private sector, as shown in Table 2-1.

It will be seen from the table that the nomenclature of sectors differs somewhat from that adopted by Thailand, but there are broad similarities. The broader social sector is dealt with by the Ceylon plan under the heading of social overheads, but presumably the total investment for social overheads is included under the various other headings in the table. The plan criticizes past investment in education and says "judging from results it is no exaggeration to say that the social returns to educational investment had been negligible, if not negative." The unrelatedness of the curricula to economic and social realities comes in for particular complaint. This is then reflected in the specific targets for the educational subsector. These are:

1. The development of the curricula required for the changes envisaged in the educational system.
2. The phased introduction of new curricula commencing from Grade 6 in 1972.
3. The upgrading of schools throughout the country to remove the imbalance in the distribution of educational facilities and the equipping of selected

Table 2-1
Breakdown of Expenditures in Ceylon's Five Year Plan 1971-1976
(In Millions of Rupees at Current Prices)

	Total	Public	Private
Agriculture	3,000	1,700	1,300
Industry	2,240	1,240	1,000
Transport, Communications and Power	2,480	2,290	190
Services	850	550	300
Construction			
Housing	4,200	200	4,000
Other	100	60	40
Capital Replacements	1,000	500	500
Total gross fixed investments	13,870	6,540	7,330
Addition to stocks and work in progress	950	500	450
Total gross investment	14,820	7,040	7,780

schools in the regions to develop and adapt the curricula and teaching material to implement the changes.

4. Intensive teacher training and inservice training to equip the present cadres for improving the quality of education at the primary and secondary levels.

5. Special programs for expanding and improving the teaching of English as a second language and the establishment of a separate training college for the training of English teachers.

6. Diversification of higher education by enlarging the scope of applied studies that are especially relevant to the country's development needs.

For each of these targets the plan provides for programs and projects designed to achieve the ends proposed. Thus there is a program for diversifying the country's higher education, composed of projects for new courses and disciplines. There is a program for intensifying teacher training and inservice training. Similarly, the program to expand and improve the teaching of English as a second language includes a special project for the establishment of a separate training college for training teachers of English.

These examples are from only two countries in the region, but the intention is to provide a general picture of the usual approach to national planning and to give some idea of the way in which the operation is normally developed in practice. National plans will tend to follow the patterns given, if only because when formulating anything as serious as a national plan, one country tends to borrow from the others. Furthermore, in the developing areas of the world the advisers on national planning have tended to come from similar backgrounds or be provided by the United Nations, World Bank, or multilateral and bilateral aid, the personnel of which are acquainted with each other's work. Also the indigenous planners have tended to seek training in foreign institutions, which approach the problem of planning in ways that generally result in a framework similar to the examples above. There exists, therefore, the mold of a common, or more or less common, academic discipline with a relatively small world club of acknowledged experts.

Finally, it is clear that the economic and social structure of a country imposes a pattern of approach that tends to divide sectors and allocate resources according to the examples given. Nevertheless, it should not be imagined that because a format has common features or because several plans have similar lines of approach they are the same. The direction a plan will take, the priorities adopted, and the detail of its execution will vary from country to country. In fact, the information already reviewed above shows that Ceylon did not follow Thailand or Thailand, Ceylon. Their aims and purposes diverged according to their own conceptions of their needs—however much the framework of the plans showed similarities.

Terminology

Already in this planning outline terms like targets, sectors, programs, projects, resources, and allocations have been used. These are the current terms of planning and will be quite familiar to those already engaged in this kind of work. Even those who are not so involved in the process of planning will have no difficulty understanding the meaning from general usage or from the context in which they are applied here. To avoid any possible misunderstanding, however— and even at the risk of laboring the obvious—it might be useful to explain that *targets* are the objectives, goals, or aims of the total plan and/or of particular parts of the plan; that the *sectors* are the separate areas or subdivisions of the economy covered by the plan, like agriculture, industry, commerce, health, education, etc.; and that *projects* and *programs* within these different sectors are the specific activities or groups of distinct operations to which the plan is allocating the nation's human, natural, and physical resources (i.e., those existing and available, or those anticipated in the plan period). *Projects* are the actual work schemes—the lowest denominators into which a plan can be subdivided. They are the molecules of the plan structure. *Programs*, on the other hand, are combinations or strings of related projects—usually within a defined sector. Thus a new school might be a construction project, but a number of these projects coupled with a training project for teachers and scholarships for students could constitute a program for extending primary or secondary education. Or the concept of projects and programs could be wider—say, a credit scheme for a countrywide organization of cooperatives could be regarded as a project, and this broad project could be linked with others, e.g., for the provision of farm equipment, animal husbandry, crop improvement, and training, to comprise a national program of agricultural improvement, which would be a special feature of a development plan.

Sometimes in seeking to reach goals or objectives planning borrows from the military vocabulary and talks of *strategies* for achieving objectives or *tactics* that might be used. Depending upon the way in which such terms are used, strategy might be sectoral, subsectoral, or conceived so broadly as to extend over several 5-year plan periods. Similarly, tactics can refer to the procedure for carrying out a given policy either within, between, or across sectors—or may again be used more widely and in a broader perspective by referring to total plans as procedures. Then the meaning of these terms will depend on the context.

Each country differs in some way in its approach to national planning, but generally speaking, wherever there is a national plan the outline of its preparation and implementation follows that of Figure 2-1.

Once again, it must be stressed that this is no more than a skeleton of the possible planning procedures. And skeletons fleshed out generally assume

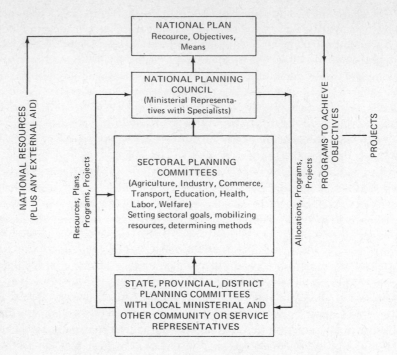

Figure 2-1. General National Planning Outline.

different features. Some countries will omit some of the steps shown here, others will have the planning councils and committees within a central planning ministry responsible for most of the operations shown above. Some countries will place more emphasis on the planning of work at local levels and will tend to decentralize, while others will strengthen the central control.

Social Planning

It is a little out of date to divide economic and social planning. Economists, in any case, have usually denied that they were dealing only with material gain, since their ultimate aims have always been happier, healthier, more competent, and more efficient people. They have maintained that they were social planners as well as economic planners. In the realm of planning, however, the facts have been largely against them. Although there have usually been obeisances to a more wholesome and happier life in the preambles to the plans, or even in the statements of objectives, these have been decidedly very long term; in the short or intermediate term the stress has been largely economic.

Of course there have been important excursions into social planning by notable economists, e.g., Pigou with his "welfare economics" concept or Keynes who provided so much of the impetus to the remedy for pre-World War II unemployment. However, incomes have been regarded as the key to satisfaction, and apart from those already mentioned the substance of plans has been distinctively economic. Production has been paramount, and in the very early years of development planning, sectors like welfare or law and order have been totally excluded as unproductive. Indeed, it was only because health and education were already very firmly established as benefits that people definitely wanted—perhaps even regardless of anything else—that these were brought into the plans and even then, always as contributing to the productiveness of labor. It was a healthier, better informed and more skillful labor force that was the aim. Thus the predominance of economics was well sustained, and economists often moved into health and education to do the necessary planning. Social values were quantified so that the number of schools, school places, hospitals, or hospital beds per head of population became measures of social well-being. Nearly all plans revealed a deep commitment to the economic or commercial sectors before any others. Social planning was not neglected, if we put health, education, or labor into this category. But, without any doubt, *social welfare planning* and *crime prevention planning* were usually treated extremely casually and often totally excluded from development planning. The human factor in the whole process of planning received minimal attention. This is not really surprising when it is remembered that the specialists doing the planning had little knowledge or experience in either social welfare or crime prevention. They had been trained to regard these as simple functions of investment and incomes. Even justice in distribution received inadequate attention.

Social planning developed, therefore, out of a need increasingly demonstrated by the inadequacies of earlier plans. In the developed countries where national planning was not so comprehensive, the need for better social investments emerged from the failures of physical planning. New towns or residential areas failed to develop communities because of the sheer unhappiness of people forced to occupy quarters that crushed their individuality and created more social problems than they solved. In the developing areas the obvious creation of one problem by solving another (e.g., lowering the infant mortality rate called for more schools, and more educated people required jobs to suit them, which in an agriculturally dependent country might not exist) made it obvious that social planning had to have a greater prominence in national planning. The realization that social problems, including crime, might be symptoms of profound dysfunctions in society or an outgrowth of human and cultural divisions and conflicts that more money and more material security might not always resolve was a realization that came slowly.

Obviously, the economic and social sectors are not entirely separable. Agriculture requires community development no less than education needs to be related to agriculture where it is the only source of employment opportunities. Therefore, the economic and social issue was largely resolved by both aspects being merged in general planning.

Today it is more appropriate to refer to planners without asking whether they are social or economic planners. Even so, these more general professions are still largely recruited from people with economic or physical backgrounds, so that some attention needs to be given to separating the social issues. The emphasis and pressure for social planning has resulted from the experience of trying to plan for the developing countries.

In socialist countries, the social planning is known and quite comprehensive, but by ideological definition it is subsumed in the economic planning—for the social conditions are held to flow from economic structures. Western societies have extensive social legislation and have evolved social policies of a public and political nature, but social planning, as such, at either the regional or national levels has not been much in evidence. In developing countries on the other hand, social planning has been called forth to meet two serious requirements that have become increasingly evident as national planning has developed and as the results of the earlier planning exercises have become available for evaluation.

The first need is obviously for a balance of investments between economic and social sectors. As mentioned, a distinction of this kind is artificial, for no economic sector is without its social side and no social sector is without its economic implication and significance. However, the planners have in the past been in the habit of stressing the "productive" sectors, like agriculture, forestry, industry, and commerce, leaving the other sectors to make their own way with limited support, until such time as the productive investments begin to yield fruit in increased output leading to increased incomes and better standards of living for all. Even the education, health, and labor, which were not neglected, had to be justified as economically significant—health and education supplying and improving the human resources for increased production—and labor ensuring the greater cooperation of workers in the productive effort. Gradually, however, experience showed that even if production increased, the spending on health resulted in more mouths to feed, more children to educate, and more dependent people in society to be maintained. Moreover, expenditure on education often resulted in educating people out of employment opportunities—maybe reducing production in agriculture where labor was needed and creating serious unemployment and political problems in the towns to which the newly educated flocked either to extend their education or to seek the white collar jobs which now seemed a human right, given the type of education they had received in schools with curricula modelled after the industrialized West. Everywhere the need for balancing economic with social investments made itself felt, and more constructive, realistic, and effective social allocations were obviously required.[d]

[d]For instance, the United Nations Expert Group on Social Policy and Planning, held from 1-10 September 1969 in Stockholm, took the view that the emphasis on accelerating growth

For this it seemed that social planners would be needed who were not merely economic planners concentrating on social problems but planners with sufficient knowledge and experience of both economic principles and realities in the social services to identify, or even formulate, the kind of programs and projects that would have the most far-reaching effects and promote national progress.

The second call for social planners came as a result of a growing realization that plans for developing countries built on Western concepts of human behavior and motivation would not necessarily work in all other cultures. The fact that value systems differed fundamentally (e.g., farmers sometimes preferred time to income or methods of cultivation that had religious or spiritual significances to the new technologies) had to be acknowledged. All this had to be added to the growing experience that some of the most modern techniques were inappropriate to different geographical and cultural conditions (e.g., bulldozers might be less efficient than ordinary manpower as they depended on supplies or spare parts which could not be ensured or were not locally available); planners became increasingly aware that cooperatives might not work in areas with little experience of a money economy, or that the brain drain might rob a project of its best operators at the most crucial point of time, or that the social changes induced by purely economic investments (e.g., in industry) could produce family or social group changes leading to conflicts, resistances, and problems likely to impede material progress or reduce expected output. Moreover, the social problems of crime and juvenile delinquency, matrimonial disruption, prostitution, shanty towns, malnutrition, or bad housing were having profound effects on the economy—and to this could be added the maldistribution of the benefits of increased production in countries with social structures too unjust for the majority of those making the effort to obtain appreciable rewards.

Thus by 1967-1968, the need for social planners was making itself felt—although these planners were not yet being trained by the universities and institutes. Sectoral planners were emerging, however; there were already health planners, educational planners, and manpower planners becoming better known. But still, specialist courses for these forms of professional activity were difficult to find. The more general social planner was even more rare. From then till now, the felt need for social planners has gradually increased but has been most conspicuously unfilled. A definite profession of social planners has not yet emerged in the developed countries, i.e., as distinct from economic or general planning. Nor have social planners effectively emerged in the developing countries—although there are now signs that specialists in the field may be emerging in some of the developing countries with strong plan organizations, like Iran, India, or maybe Thailand.

of national income in preparation for the United Nations Second Development Decade neglected many of the developing countries problems, such as the dualist social structure, inequalities, and unemployment of human potential. The fact that development in a country often either leaves behind, or in some ways, even creates large areas of poverty, stagnation, marginality, and actual exclusion from economic and social progress was felt by the Group to require urgent consideration in the strategy for development.

Because the need for social planning is so great, the supply of social planners so small, and the shape of the subject so amorphous, all types of professionals are becoming involved in different levels of social planning. Sociologists and, especially, applied sociologists are prominent in urban and regional planning. Economists with a social bent still dominate the national levels, but social workers, social anthropologists, social administrators, and public administrators are moving in. Sometimes these persons are involved in those industrialized countries without central planning agencies in the various approaches used to inject a planning perspective into the regular process of annual budgeting.[7] Sometimes they are active in urban renewal programs or regional planning. And sometimes they are associated with attempts to rationalize social investments.[e]

That social planning needs economic support and will totally collapse without it is fully understood. When incomes fall, or unemployment comes, or inflation makes salaries or pensions inadequate, the economic factor is well understood. Good community life is difficult to enjoy without subsistence. St. Thomas Aquinas taught that man's duty was to feed the hungry with food before teaching them philosophy or theology. The efforts that nearly all social services—official or voluntary—make to raise funds is another constant reminder of the economic character of social needs. The reverse is not true, however. The essential social content of economic development is not always quite so obvious. The importance of human relations, culture, and confidence in obtaining economic well-being is not fully understood and is often ignored in plans and programs. Some of the ways that social planning becomes important, when economic growth is under consideration, have already been touched upon, however, they are worth spelling out.

First, social problems are not always simple outgrowths of economic problems. People will sometimes die of hunger rather than eat what is taboo. In Africa a partially educated person has more status when unemployed but still regarded as an unemployed student awaiting education than he is likely to have if he accepts manual work. Racial discrimination can survive and disrupt great development in all sectors. Secondly, there are obvious social requirements for any economic growth. Economic development depends *inter alia* upon there being a healthy and productive labor force, properly educated to contribute to development in an increasingly technological age. This means that social investments in health, education, and welfare may be necessary concomitants to any attempt to expand production and improve the GNP and national income. But, far beyond this, economic growth depends upon motivation, which in turn may derive from cultural values, a political need for recognition, or the kind of unity that may be difficult to inspire in a plural society.

Thirdly, social planning is necessary if it is hoped to increase resources—especially human resources. This is most often understood in its opposite sense,

[e]e.g. developing techniques for quantifications like cost/benefit or cost/effectiveness schemes or perhaps developing studies of the costs of mental health, crime, etc.

i.e., in the well propagated need to limit populations to manageable proportions. But history has demonstrated that growth is sometimes forced by the need to feed increasing numbers—or to provide them with living space. The concept of capital can readily be expanded to include nonmaterial, as well as material, assets. And without any doubt, the most fundamental wealth of any nation is to be found in its people.[f] Investments in the health, welfare, energies, training, and the development of the various skills of a nation are investments in a nation's economic wealth or capital, as this is more widely defined to include human resources. Nor should this exclude investments in the kind of social structure and character development that prevents crime. Thus, it is significant that there are correlations between education, nutrition, and health levels and the growth of the GNP. Whether this amounts to a direct causal relationship may yet be in doubt, but the correlations indicate that one cannot afford to neglect the obvious association. It has been discovered, for instance, that only a small part of the economic growth in Western industrialized nations can be attributed to the conventional inputs of capital and labor; and it has been argued, though perhaps still not proved conclusively, that the "residual factor" to which economic growth can be attributed is the input in the health and education of the labor force. How far this analysis is applicable to other countries is still debatable, and no doubt local cultures, institutions, and patterns of living need to be taken into account. Nevertheless, in light of the evidence available, it would be short-sighted for any economic planner to overlook the need for a balance between the capital, technology, or land available and the level of social progress.

Still looking at the purely economic value of social investments, one must include the many social obstacles to development that must be surmounted if material progress is to be possible. Experience has shown that even the most ambitious, scientifically designed forms of economic development are likely to flounder if the local cultural values and patterns of life are ignored. It cannot be assumed that people everywhere will necessarily react to higher incomes or industrial ways of living as they have done in the West. The Japanese offer a good example of progress within a social context very different from that of the West. In fact, most of the economic progress in Japan might be due to Japan's use of its basic social structure to obtain growth with relative stability—the lesson is there for any economic planner to learn.

If, therefore, one is thinking only of the great need for economic growth, the importance of the social investments cannot be omitted. The social side of economic development is crucial to increased production and efficient distribution. However, it would be a serious mistake to suppose that social investments

---

[f]However, the new drive to control population growth in so many parts of the world indicates a belief that the wealth of human resources is in quality rather than quantity. Too many people can result in such pressure on other available resources that development efforts cannot keep pace.

need any economic justification. Whether health and education are economically useful or not, they are valuable ends in themselves for any plan that hopes to increase the well-being of the people. People will demand medical services and increased education whether or not they are economically justifiable. They are ends in themselves, requiring economic as well as social means for achievement. After all, a plan aims at increasing production only because of the better way of life that extra material resources can buy. Indeed, it may well be argued that economic investments are themselves only justifiable if they can ensure better social conditions for the populace. This is now becoming a more popular way of looking at planning in the developed countries, where environmental pollution and the great social disadvantages of the drive for material wealth are beginning to make themselves felt.

There are at least two ways of looking at forms of planning, therefore. Where an increase in the rate of economic growth is considered as the main aim, the social variables may be conceived as conditions, constraints, or obstacles to economic growth. Conversely, when the objectives are reconceived in social terms and the aims are to obtain specified socially desirable changes, it becomes the economic resources (or the lack of them) that are the restraints, or impediments, to progress. It all depends upon the side of the social coin one has in view when considering a plan and its purpose.

It is important to ask, therefore, what the objectives of social planning are. This is a bigger question than can be fully considered here, but it should be noted (in words at any rate) that national plans have usually had long-term objectives that were unexceptionable in social terms and could well be adopted by most social planners. To paraphrase these objectives, the national plans prepared so far have frequently declared themselves to be aiming at higher incomes, public welfare, and a fuller life for everyone. These are broad, satisfying, and totally acceptable social objectives in any country. So it can be said that most national plans begin with acceptable *long-term* social objectives. In fact these objectives, as stated, are usually so broadly desirable that they would be difficult for anyone to criticize. Like virtue, everyone is for them—at least until it becomes apparent what they really mean in concrete terms. And with most plans, these objectives have been left without concrete interpretation—they have been left very much in the air. Having expressed such highly desirable aims as long-term objectives, the plans published so far have usually proceeded to leave aside the whole question of the long term and settle down in their tables, charts, strategies, and programs—the detailed provisions for the short term. And in this shorter period, it is the productive or economic investments that tend to dominate national action, in order to produce that improvement in total production and income that apparently makes it more reasonable and realistic to talk of the social improvements scheduled for the longer term.

Meanwhile, apart from considerable improvements in education, health, and labor (justified on the economic ground explained above), most social investments were to be regarded as luxuries that could be ill afforded in the short term. More particularly, expenditure on social problems, like crime or family disruption, was likely to be particularly wasteful, since it would tend to attract resources from the longer-term solutions based on better incomes for all.

The difficulty here is that this economically oriented short term shows a marked tendency to protract itself, so that for a generation or more one has heard little beyond the importance of productive investments. Now that (in the developed countries, at any rate) the limitations of the mainly productive approach are being realized, the opportunities missed in the past by not taking the social problems into account are coming to light. Evaluation of the effects on populations now serves to show what better qualitative results might have been obtained had more of the social needs been taken into account earlier.

Therefore, the first point to make about the objective of social planning is that it seeks to spread the emphasis on social aims from the longer to the shorter term. One of its intentions is to underline the interrelatedness of economic and social situations and to show that in the short term as well as the long term they need to be taken together. Secondly, social planning tries to balance the importance of increased output with the importance of equitable distribution, full employment, and things like decent housing and a mitigation of social problems—including the prevention of crime. In this respect it not only makes social objectives the real measure of both the economic and social plan but also seeks to demonstrate that even economic means are likely to be limited without attention being paid to their social dimensions. Thirdly, social planning is intended to balance the drives of social investments themselves. Health, education, and welfare are all desirable in their own right, and they need no economic justification as we have seen. They cannot be all-out objectives all the time without reference to one another. When out of proportion, any one of them can deflate the others. There can be no end to health, education, or welfare expenditures, simply because each of these has no ceiling. Since resources are never unlimited, it is obvious that we cannot always have all the health support that is desirable, all the education we would like, or all the welfare needed without end. A proportion between them is usually necessary, and this proportion is the task of social planning. Fourthly, it must be noted (though it cannot be fully discussed here) that social planning has obvious political dimensions. The above sketch of possible aims leaves no doubt that the social planner is a person who necessarily finds himself involved in serving certain basic principles or values. These are social values, but like all such standards or precepts, they have obvious political implications.

Planners have been experimenting recently with possible changes in some of the indicators used to measure progress—so as to take account of the increasing criticism of purely physical or material counting. If, for example, the GNP were not only a measure of goods and services produced but also a measure of the flow of incomes and the increases in the stocks of housing, factories, and public facilities, it would more adequately indicate the status of a nation. Usually the GNP is expressed monetarily, but it might be adjusted to include housing, the teacher-student ratio, the amount of road paving, and the number of water systems per household. There are already some nonmonetary indicators of progress in use, such as nutrition conditions expressed in calories, infant mortality rates, morbidity rates, the number of labor hours reduced, the accidental death rate, etc. There is still a problem of aggregating these figures, since one is trying to count unlike factors. There can of course be a weighting of all these factors, at least, to obtain comparisons between countries.

Another approach has been to change the GNP concept into a new measure of Net National Welfare—the NNW. Behind this approach is the realization that the GNP, which shows the production total of one year, i.e., total goods and services, could include some things that would not be goods at all but rather negative output. Compare, for example, the output of pornography or narcotics. These are counted in any measure of production, but the question of whether they are positive or negative for the economy is still questionable. Then again, a GNP does not usually measure the other things that industrialization produces, like garbage, waste material, traffic bottlenecks, pollution, etc. Therefore, a more realistic conception of the effects of economic progress is beginning to emerge, and it will take account of social elements and avoid the pitfalls of measuring progress either by material production (good or bad) only or by quantities only.

In March 1973 the Net National Welfare Measurement Committee of Japan's Economic Council reported on its attempt to develop a new indicator of economic welfare (NNW), by means of modifying the present national income concepts by adding and subtracting positive or negative factors measured in monetary terms. Since the concept of NNW had to include factors that would not reflect effective demand (in the economic sense), such as leisure and the nonmarket activities of housewives, the committee pointed out that NNW would probably not provide an adequate analytical tool for use in econometric models that measure the effects of changes in effective demand. "Therefore," said the committee "it is not correct to expect NNW to take the place of GNP." Rather it is intended to be a parallel measure of welfare.[8]

Included in the NNW were such things as government consumption, which included government expenditures on health, education, culture, and social welfare, all of which had a welfare augmenting nature. But, significantly, judicial and police administration as well as the costs of correctional services were excluded, because they were taken to be *defensive* in nature. Similarly there was great emphasis placed upon the determination of levels of pollution, traffic accidents, deductions of commuting expenses, funeral costs, and business and ceremonial expenses, but there was no mention of crime losses.

Currently, however, Japan is experimenting with a measurement of public safety, and a Tokyo committee is trying to determine the minimum levels of public safety that people wish to enjoy—and which might therefore become a goal quantifier for future planning.

Notes

1. Naomi Caiden and Aaron Wildavsky, *Planning and Budgeting in Poor Countries* (New York: John Wiley and Sons, 1974).

2. C.S. Alfonso, *Organization for Economic Planning: The National Economic Council, the Presidential Economic Staff, the Budget Commission, and the Central Bank*; and *Perspectives in Government Reorganization*, ed. J.V. Abveva (Manila: University of Philippines, 1969).

3. John Michael Montian, "Economic Planning: Eastern Europe," in *International Encyclopedia of Social Sciences*, ed. David L. Sills (New York: The Macmillan Company and the Free Press, 1968), p. 110.

4. Ibid., p. 111.

5. A. Premchand, "Budgetary Process in State Governments," *Indian Journal of Public Administration*, 13, 4 December 1967, as quoted in Caiden and Wildavsky, op. cit., p. 90.

6. Caiden and Wildavsky, op. cit., p. 178.

7. See W. Gorham, *Sharpening the Knife that Cuts the Public Pie*, especially IV on "Planning and Budgetary Decisions." *Congressional Record* 5 December 1967, pp. 17861-6.

8. *NNW: Report of the NNW Measurement Committee*, Japanese Ministry of Finance, 1973.

3

Crime Prevention Planning

Planning and Implementation

It is abundantly clear that, in both developed and developing areas, crime has not been recognized, until very recently, as the serious drain on the economy and widespread distortor of the distribution of the real benefits of development that it undoubtedly is. The tendency to regard crime as a particular behavioral, or a distinctly social, problem far removed from ordinary life and the basic issues of economic and social progress has persisted far too long. It has resulted in the valuing of any kind of material progress or any improvements in individual wealth or acquisitions for their own sake, regardless of how antisocial or morally reprehensible the methods were by which progress was achieved or wealth acquired. Methods, however, effect development.

The Prime Minister of Thailand in his budget speech for 1971 said:

The government regards that economic development will proceed smoothly when our people are able to pursue gainful livelihood and abide in peace, free from criminal attempts to harm and rob. The total appropriation for this amounts to 1,898.2 million baht of which the main portion will be allocated to the Police Department, which will expand its strength by another 5,100 policemen. . . . [1]

Here, the recognition that economic development is dependent upon personal and property security is more laudable than the assumption that the only way to attain this is by having more policemen. The limitations of simply adding to police, prisons, and courts as a means of controlling crime are dealt with more fully below. It is the assumption underlying the Thailand plan that is exposed here. It may be added, however, that a paper produced for the United Nations Social Defence Planning Meeting in November 1975 showed that despite substantial increases in the police forces in Thailand, crime has been increasing at a rate of 3.8 percent per annum as opposed to the natural population growth of 3.1 percent per annum. Property crimes and sex offenses had shown marked increases.

From another angle, the more recent studies of the costs of crime in some countries have begun to show that crime is not only an obstacle to development but also can be a tremendous loss to the economy. There is a loss not simply in the disturbance to regular production occasioned by the stealing, violence, or the diversion of staff from production to crime control. It is incurred also in the nullifying of government levies and controls by multinational operations and in the undermining of the security and confidence on which the total system depends. More particularly, it occurs in the illegal diversion of assets and incomes to the undeserving pockets of criminals—and, above all, in the less calculable but equally damaging undermining of the security and confidence on which any economy depends.[a] It also costs in terms of increased insurance premiums, payments of special security services, alarms, burglary prevention devices, locks, bars, guard dogs, and fences.

If crime is so much of an obstacle to, and a debilitation of, the economy, then not only the growth but the maintenance of the economy depends upon the process of planning (whether social or economic) taking account of the need to plan for less crime. It is as necessary as disease prevention is to health—quite apart from the need to reduce the misery, tragedy, and suffering associated with crime. But, however logical, it was not until recently that the significance of crime prevention services was recognized not only in the promotion of social order and social justice but also in the productive and necessary protection of commerce, industry, and the economy generally and/or a contributor to increased welfare and social improvement. With this realization has come a new demand for crime prevention planning specialists—a new profession within the general boundary of economic and social planning concerned with the rationalization of the expenditures on crime and their effective, humane, and just use.

In planning, therefore, crime prevention is a new sector, just beginning to earn recognition as an area worthy of specialist attention. The extension and scope of the subject is important. To be effective it must cover not only the criminal justice system and all the planning required for the future development of the police, prisons, courts, parole, probation, and reformative institutions as an integrated crime prevention mechanism in itself, but also it must logically extend less directly to those aspects of education, health, labor, welfare, agriculture, industry, and other sectors of the economy that have obvious relevance for crime production as well as crime prevention. In this sense, crime prevention planning, while comprising an identifiable group of services that can be grouped as a sector, permeates all other areas of the economy. There is no part of the social and economic system insulated against crime—and if corruption, white-collar crime, narcotics, piracy, and cultural crime are included, it is quite obvious that no part of national and international life really escapes its concern.

It should not be thought, however, that the crime prevention sector is unusual in having this two-dimensional character, i.e., one part specific to itself

---

[a]It should be observed, however, that crime is not all economic loss. The sum total of thefts, for example, could, and sometimes does, represent in a country an efficient transfer of resources. It might concentrate wealth (even in criminal hands) for legal, productive investment. And if this movement of wealth by crime is from an idle rich to an economically active poor, it might even benefit a community. Moreover, even from the earliest times crime has been recognized as a possible agent of social and political change.

and another part extending into other sectors. Much the same could be claimed by any one of the other sectors. Education, besides its interest in schools and its preoccupation with formal school services, has an obvious and definite concern with all the other aspects of the life of a country which have educational implications. Thus it claims a share of involvement in all kinds of cultural or informal learning activities, publications, trade training programs, and media programs that have educational implications or consequences, even though these are sometimes far removed from the regular or formal school system. Similarly, health is the concern of many more than those actually working in Ministries of Health, following, as it does, the process of human growth and development wherever and however it occurs. So the treatment of crime prevention both as a distinctive sector in planning and as an aspect of all other sectors is justifiable and in accordance with the perspectives usually adopted for other parts of the national economy.

From the dichotomy between developmental and ordinary budgets that was described above, there derived a dichotomy of thinking. Regular expenditures and investments in productive land capital or labor for future growth seemed to be quite separate—there appeared, indeed, a possibility of losing the development thrust if development funds got lost in the regular budget, so dominated by salaries that it left little room for maneuver. So when development planning as a national activity began to attract more attention, when planning officers or planning ministries were established, crime prevention not only belonged to another budget, the regular budget, but it belonged conceptually to another world. Consequently, none of the possibly criminogenic elements in agriculture, forestry, housing, and communications were considered in the large-scale investments. Even the obvious opportunities for corruption and the mismanagement of funds when large development investments were being made were ignored or neglected completely; or else they were discounted as calculated risks that were part of the costs of the various programs and projects. Crime prevention was just not a subject for the development planners—and even now it gets precious little attention.

There are some indications that this may be changing, but whether it will ever take adequate account of crime prevention needs in the totality of development planning will depend greatly upon the guidance that planners with training in crime prevention might be able to provide.

The Objectives of Crime Prevention Planning

From the eighteenth century concern with prison reform, there arose some very idealistic conceptions of the aims and objectives of crime prevention—especially its correctional features. Gustave de Beaumont and Alexis de Tocqueville writing "On the Penitentiary System in the United States" quoted at least one person who hoped that the day would come when "all the wicked having been regenerated, prisons would be no longer wanted." The authors were properly skeptical of this idealistic concept of human nature and quoted this remark only to criticize it. Moreover, we no longer equate crime and sin to the extent that was done in the early days of penal reform. Nevertheless, in some rehabilitation programs—or even in the more recent programs for law and order—it is not difficult to find reflections of a pious hope that there can be a golden future in which crime will be nonexistent.

The hope that prisons can someday be eliminated may not be postulated, today, on the increasing perfection of human nature but rather is more likely to come from the demand for an increasing tolerance of the imperfections of human nature (the right to be different or deviant) but the hope is still that we will not need prisons and can manage without the desire to control each other's behavior. We have not yet outgrown the simple faith that suitable measures can be taken either to make man perfect or to create a society in which the imperfections will be so tolerated that there will be no need for a criminal justice system. The fact is, however, that crime in some form, even though differently interpreted, tends to persist and to outlive utopias. A perfect society would have some people less perfect than others, who might threaten the continuance of perfection; and a society of gangsters would, if experience can be a guide, have iron discipline and harsh sanctions for those daring to break the code. History has demonstrated that as a practical objective for crime prevention, the perfecting of a man or his society is rarely acceptable and never realistic. Crime is a relative concept, and we have evidence of societies all along the continuum of complexity and ideological conviction using police, courts, and correctional services.

Today it is usual to accept crime as perennial in one form or another and to formulate the objective of crime prevention planning[b] as the *reduction* of total crime in a country. This may be imprecise, but it is not impracticable. No state is likely to be able to eliminate crime altogether. By definition there will always be some forms of deviation from any established norms. Whether or not these deviations are going to be called crime is really a matter of policy and terminology. On the other hand, freedom of any kind must include the freedom to decide whether to keep or break the law. A totally regulated society in which everyone is so strictly supervised and directed that the possibility of breaking the law is totally excluded may be possible, but it would not be human. Societies always have problems of unacceptable behavior, therefore it might be said that no crimeless society exists and that it is unwarrantably idealistic to prefer crime elimination as an aim of crime prevention planning. This is especially true if we hope to preserve, at the same time, a measure of individual and group consideration.

Although the reduction of the total incidence of crime is rather less

---

[b]Or criminal justice planning, see below.

objectionable as a goal for crime prevention planners, it must be admitted that it still has an unfortunately negative connotation. Crime prevention planning is not *for* something but *against* something. It is more difficult to avoid this, however, than it is to justify it. And it is easy to place it in a similar category to the preventative aims of health services. Preventative medicine is negative, but it is obviously in the service of better health. Crime prevention is in the service of a better kind of society. We try to reduce the incidence of malaria, tuberculosis, cancer, and coronary occlusion, and we do not regard such objectives as unacceptable for planning. Crime reduction would be similar in its scope and implications.

Nevertheless, if one cannot be specific enough to say how much of a reduction is to be sought within a given time, then it is very much a vague goal, subject to all the criticism that has been levelled in the past against unrealistic or vague objectives. On the other hand, with crime growing in most countries, it could well be argued that *any* reduction in crime would be an achievement. In this sense reduction even without specification is a meaningful objective. We frequently aim in national planning at a reduction of traffic accidents, outflows of foreign reserves, or at a reduction of population (in the new population limitation campaigns); and the new concern with the environment leads to planning for less pollution. The reduction of crime need not therefore be excluded entirely because of its defects of imprecision and negation.

The crime prevention planner might wish, nevertheless, to begin by seeking a more positive frame of reference, by looking for a more creative role for his total planning effort. In the widest and most general sense, he can borrow his long-term objectives from those of the national plan itself—and indeed it is necessary that he do so in order for his plan to become an integrated part of the total planning operation. It would not be difficult for a crime prevention planner to adopt, for example, the broad aims of the Ceylon Five Year Plan 1972-1976, which were to provide employment, to "bridge the present disparities in incomes and living standards . . . (and) . . . to eliminate the grosser forms of wasteful consumption." All these could be crime preventative in the sense that if neglected, they could be expected to protract conditions that might be criminogenic. Similarly, the Third National Economic and Social Development Plan for Thailand specifies such objectives as the reduction of income disparities, the promotion of social justice, and the creation of employment—all of which are perfectly acceptable crime prevention principles. Both the social planner and the crime prevention planner will be looking for a fuller life for all citizens—and, by this, they mean *inter alia* an existence untroubled by insecurity, free of the fear of violent attack, undisturbed by extortion and exploitation, and emancipated from all the constraints that increasing and increasingly serious crime impose on the ordinary flow of human activities.

The crime prevention planner will want to improve incomes and housing to reduce poverty, extend the nation's productive capacity to create jobs, and reduce unemployment so as to discourage the offenses that flow from social conditions, social injustice, and inequalities. He will also want to promote the better health of the population and develop more meaningful lifestyles for personal fulfillment so as to reduce those crimes connected with physical or mental disorders. Even the achievement of good trade balances can both serve the general good of the economy and reduce incentives for economic crime or currency offenses, while the greater equality of distribution can reduce the familiar frustrations of limited opportunities leading to illegal shortcuts to power and status. All these are factors that if not causes, are frequent concomitants of crime; and they certainly cannot be regarded as irrelevant to crime prevention planning. If a shorthand expression is needed to provide a succinct objective for crime prevention that takes account of all this, it could be "more development with less crime" or "the elimination of criminogenic obstacles to growth." These are economically related objectives that avoid the negative connotations of crime reduction, but they are still broad objectives in need of more precise presentation. They are still in need of the kind of concretization that makes a plan realistic. They have to be reduced to detail and to shorter form so that they become aims whose achievement can be measured, or at least evaluated, objectively.

The reduction of the longer-term objectives to these shorter-term targets and goals still permits the crime prevention planner to be as positive as he is negative. He need not allow his preoccupation with a single social problem like crime shift his perspectives. He can still work for a more wholesome shift of perspectives. He can still work for a more wholesome society rather than limiting his sights to purely negative counteraction. Dealing with crime—if it means anything at all—certainly means helping people socialize more effectively and incorporate in themselves the values of the wider society. If these values are clear and largely unchallenged as, for example, in a Moslem society, in an avowed socialist system, or in a state with persisting family loyalties like Japan, then the crime prevention planner's task is easier. In a mobile, uncertain, or changing society where behavioral standards are dynamic and where individual and social values are numerous, unrelated, and often conflicting, the crime prevention planner has a formidable task, which he cannot be expected to deal with alone. It is made more difficult wherever the really fundamental values are not uniformly accepted, are undecided or unstable, or are in a state of flux. Nevertheless, if the present state of world knowledge of crime prevention can be interpreted into practical policies, it surely means that dealing with crime involves a strengthening and expanding of community life and a fostering of that kind of community participation that evolves and maintains the informal social controls which sustain order and which render more formal law enforcement largely unnecessary.

Frequently, the shorter-term objectives are reduced to the simple formula of "law and order." Ordinarily this could be accepted as a positive condition of any society and one that any good government should be aiming at; but the terms *law and order* have been politically infected. In some states, it has been the label attached to sternly repressive action to stifle all dissent in defense of the status quo. It has unfortunately been the rallying cry of the worst as well as the best governments faced with dissident populations; and because of its abuse by unworthy causes, it does not have the appeal that it undoubtedly merits. Thus the crime prevention planner who hopes to mobilize widespread public support and avoid controversy is probably deprived, in many parts of the world, of this valuable short-term objective.

In some of the great urban areas where night attacks are endemic, housebreakings rife, or robberies frequent, the restoration of security might be a suitable pseudonym for the action that any crime prevention planner will be aiming at in the short term. The need will be to restore confidence. And "community development" is not a bad direction to take if it is understood that this means developing a society without fears of criminal attack and depredation.

However, this discussion has not settled the question of objectives for the crime prevention sector of an economy. It could not do so because the matter is still under discussion in a number of countries. However, the principles are likely to be common as approaches are made to objectives. This brief account was intended only to provide a range of possibilities.

Obviously, the long-term or short-term objectives that a country decides to adopt will depend upon local circumstances and public interpretations of the aims proposed. The most one can say in a general discussion is that the objectives adopted should not be so unrealistic as to run the danger of becoming meaningless. They should always be amenable to evaluation and later assessment.

Targets

Once the objectives have been determined, it will be necessary for the crime prevention planner to sort out for each subsector the implications of the decisions. It is desirable to find some way of setting bench marks for each of the specific subsectors dealing directly with crime (police, prisons, courts, etc.) and also to attempt fairly specific definitions of the work to be done in the other sectors of the economy (agriculture, industry, education, health, etc.). Here it is impossible to be more precise without taking examples of a hypothetical nature, since so little work has yet been done in this field.

Supposing the objective in the short term is a "restoration of security," it would be wise to give this a dimension. It obviously cannot mean the total elimination of deviant behavior for the reasons already given. What then can it mean? Perhaps the answer would be to select some past year, say in the 1940s or 1950s when most people were untroubled by crime, and use the figures then as targets now. Obviously, such figures would need to be corrected for population changes, unemployed, etc., but a fair precision can be achieved in setting an arbitrary standard of this kind. It might not be particularly imaginative, but it can often be a rough guide to the amount of crime a society might be able to tolerate without feeling directly threatened.

Sometime a country might decide that it should, within some given period, reduce its amount of crime by a given percentage. One developed country recently decided to concentrate upon programs designed to reduce the rate of crime by 20 percent.

Failing this, a planner might decide that security could be induced by a reduction of certain specific offenses, e.g., homicide, burglary, robbery, etc. (insofar as these are reported or discovered by the authorities), by say 5 percent or 10 percent within a given period. He might aim at reducing prison committals by a given proportion or making more use of other procedures available to the authorities. He might decide to take, as his aim for the police forces, the raising of the rate of crime detection. Or he might seek adoption of a definite and specified reduction in the rate of recidivism for the correctional services. Certainly in the present imperfect state of our knowledge of crime, and with the known shortcomings of the system for collecting information, any figures of this kind will be quantifiers open to criticism and variable interpretation. Suppose, for example, that total crime is reduced by 20 percent, but this happens to be a reduction in the traffic or minor offenses rather than in serious crimes against property or against the person. Would this be a true achievement, helping to restore the population's sense of security? To take another example, the success of greater public participation in crime prevention could lead to more reports to the police, raising rather than lowering the known incidence of crime. Or again, a lowering of the recidivist rate could be complicated by a rise in the number of first convictions. Figures, therefore, are only an approximate guide and can be misleading. What is required is the use of such qualifications to evaluate progress—but to be taken alongside the qualitative data that will also be needed. Over time it is hoped that the quantitative indicators can be refined and improved to make planning more efficient.

But this complication of inadequate quantifiers is not limited to crime prevention targets. GNP figures, for instance, are also differentially compiled or interpretable, as we have already seen. And even import figures or census returns are not without their own complications. When highly sophisticated techniques for a city census can result in considerable numbers of people being uncounted (see reports of some of the censuses in developed countries), it is obvious that planning cannot always be based on impeccable data. It can only be as good as circumstances permit. Naturally, there will be difficulties with arbitrary crime prevention targets of this kind, and of course there will be challengeable interpretations whenever the results are evaluated. The point is that this should not deter the new crime prevention planner. He may take heart, if not comfort, from the fact that there are planning areas other than crime prevention that are sometimes fortunate in being able to be even this exact in their attempts at quantification.

Nevertheless, this justification of target setting is not intended to suggest that such rough and questionable quantifying is satisfactory. It can be only a first stage expedient. What are needed in the future are more refined techniques for calculating and evaluating the progress that crime prevention planning can make towards these admittedly still unsatisfactory aims and objectives.

The crime prevention planner must now think of targets for other than the direct crime prevention sectors. These will be more diffused and a good deal more subtle. To begin with, it is possible for him, perhaps, to adopt the quantified targets of other sectors. After all, if they achieve, say, a 15 percent expansion of schooling or employment, or an improvement by a stated figure in output, he might well feel that he has done his work by ensuring that crime did not interfere with this achievement.

In some areas, however, this may not be good enough. As we have seen, the investment itself could be criminogenic. If a 15 percent improvement in schooling, for example, will be likely to create a pool of unemployed, frustrated youth vulnerable to criminal propensity, then he may be making his contribution to target-setting in the education sector by bringing forward the evidence and analyzing his projections for the benefit of education planning colleagues. Maybe this would result in the education target being reduced to 10 or 12 percent, to take account of the crime producing implications.

Similarly, in these other sectors the crime prevention planner will have to do studies of the rates of wastage or loss through theft or crime that are oncosted in the calculation of target figures. His own targets in these sectors could be related to a reduction in the amount that has to be discounted because of expected crime or negligence. The amounts discounted by industry, retailers, or libraries to account for stealing are sometimes enormous and could well be reduced by better planning.

Finally, there will be targets without necessary reference to fair or just distribution of the benefits in these other sectors. Here the crime prevention planner, apart from ensuring that corruption and crime do not syphon off the profits, will be interested in seeing that funds or rewards end up where originally intended. Here he can set targets related to the sectoral planning of these objectives.

One interesting attempt to reduce crime indirectly has been adopted by a local newspaper in an urban area of Victoria, Australia. The newspaper is mounting a campaign to reduce the number of deaths and injuries on the roads. Given the latest figures, the public is then asked to cooperate in preventing increases and, eventually, in reducing the toll. The effect is not yet available, but the method foreshadows the planning approach suggested here.

Programs

When objectives and targets have been specified, not only for the crime prevention sector but for all the subsectors, the various programs required to realize these targets and achieve these objectives will have to be formulated. Here it must be confessed that crime prevention is faced with its most formidable problem, since there is still so much uncertainty as to the factors that are causative or the remedies that are effective. Most of the research done to date is still inconclusive and subject to different interpretations. How to prevent crime is still largely in doubt.

In the first stages of planning, then, it will probably be necessary to proceed on assumptions that are at least reasonable and likely to be valid. It is clear that there is a relationship between the decline in family life and the rise in crime. It is also clear that there is a relationship between the socialization of children and their later behavior. It is evident that low crime rates and strong community ties are associated. And it is clear that recidivism will depend to a great extent upon the certainty of detection and the incidence of street crime will depend upon the amount of attention given to the organization of police patrols and the extent of street lighting. There are, therefore, a number of programs that can be drawn up to strengthen the positive elements—and if the results are carefully monitored by evaluation techniques, the research on crime causation and control will be advanced.

So in education, health, labor, and social welfare, it will be necessary to draft programs likely to have a crime prevention effect. Child care programs, designed to reduce the personality defects that lead to potentially delinquent behavior; family support programs, designed to keep families united so as to foster better child care; educational programs to improve socialization; labor programs to reduce unemployment; and programs to improve mental health and provide better care for those suffering from afflictions likely to result in antisocial behavior are all obvious requirements for effective crime prevention. Then in the more direct services, such as police, prisons, courts, probation, parole, etc., it will be necessary to provide more specific programs to deal with crime. These might include measures to increase the police efficiency, improve the training of police officers, and develop new techniques in forensic science and crime detection. This might mean new building programs to avoid the overcrowding of prisons, more extensive community alternatives or better facilities for probation and parole so as to keep more people out of the prisons, better facilities for the education and training of correctional personnel, new court procedures to expedite justice and streamline the court system, more judges and magistrates or improved methods of training court personnel, or perhaps programs to integrate and improve the entire criminal justice system including, particularly, the reform of the law itself.

It will be clear that all these programs will, of necessity, serve the overall objectives and the short-term targets. To do this they will need to be drawn together into a coordinated whole. At each stage there will have to be built-in provisions for evaluation, reassessment, and perhaps redirection of particular programs or parts of programs. It is in this linking and integrating of the range of programs that crime prevention planners have a most important role to play. Similarly, the various programs accepted by the plan will have run the gamut of scrutiny by the different levels of specialized parts of the planning process. They will have been accepted for implementation because they accord with the objectives and targets and have a higher priority than a number of competing programs.

One quite practical example of this need to draw together the different elements in crime prevention is expressed by the usefulness of having a broad committee or commission for the whole subject of crime prevention. Most countries could plan better, if an authority existed to bring together the efforts of the various ministries and agencies in the broad crime prevention field. This body would be able to help coordinate the work of the several services trying to deal with crime and elaborate future programs for progress and development. It could even out the conflicting interests and mobilize all the work toward agreed objectives of joint programs. It seems that Thailand has a committee of this kind within the Ministry of the Interior, charged with planning for the prevention of crime. The U.S.A. has its Law Enforcement Assistance Administration—a fund granting agency stimulating and guiding the work it finances in all states, universities, and municipalities.

Most countries have programs in crime prevention rather than crime prevention *plans*. With crime prevention largely excluded from the routine of development planning, each ministry concerned with crime has, as a rule, developed its own approach to the problems and has been attempting via annual budgeting or program budgeting to implement a number of programs designed to overcome the various difficulties encountered year by year.

The disconnected nature of this approach is evident from past experience. In the early 1950s, programming for correctional improvements in New Jersey was never effectively implemented because of a gradual reduction of the estimated amount of money required as other wider priorities arose and as corrections became relatively less important to the policy-makers than more general investments in mental health. Funds were steadily diverted from the proposed new correctional institutions to the provision of broader but less precise mental health facilities. The result was that in 1975 a correctional establishment built in the nineteenth century was still being used for a larger number of inmates than it was designed to accommodate, and it became the scene of riots and troubles directly attributable to its inadequacy. The present discontent with prison systems in the U.S. has derived, in part at least, from this kind of approach to crime problems.

Again in Singapore, new housing complexes, designed to improve living conditions for a large number of people, have become extortion traps for the new populations, as criminal secret societies sought to control these complexes via their local monopoly of small contractual operations. A new tenant, for instance, might not be able to hire any contractor to install windows, improve the fittings, or supply certain goods and services other than the one proposed by the secret society who was of course charging more for the work. All these housing services had to be obtained at higher costs through the illegal operations of the secret societies. In some other Asian areas, organized crime syndicates might even collect a regular extortionate rent from new householders as "protection" from theft or property damage. Once again, programming for crime prevention suffers from being unrelated to general social planning. It would have been possible to limit the activities of these illegal operators by a combination of police work and planning governmentally for the contractual work needed.

In many countries, Ministries of Justice, Home Affairs, Police, Law, or the Interior do not always see their own problems as related to more general planning, and they operate their programs relatively independently of the other branches of local and central government. However, it is becoming increasingly clear that they cannot alone either prevent crime or deal adequately with the crime committed.

Projects

As already shown, each of the many programs amounts to a string of defined, costed, and itemized projects, each with its own specified purpose. An increase in police strength would be a project, for example, one to be completed by a given time and to fulfill definite conditions spelled out in detail beforehand. Each new institution for the treatment of offenders amounts to a project that is carefully estimated, projected, and timed. Each project will have its objective specified and its plan of operations showing the progress to be expected at any given period—and it will be linked to other projects so that its contribution to the total program can be assessed.

Again, to take an example, a scheme to improve child care may resolve itself into several projects, one of which might be to increase the quality of counselling for mothers at mother and child centers. This might mean a project that includes an increase in the number of counsellors and provides for special courses in delinquency prevention to be given to all existing child care specialists. The numbers of extra workers would be calculated, and the year of their incorporation projected with the costs involved. Similarly, the extra instructors needed for the courses would be determined, and the salaries estimated. Correspondingly, the amounts needed for scholarships or course support would be included in such a project.

Thus each project is a distinct entity, with its timing and cost as well as its implications worked out in advance. No doubt in the process of preparing the plan, many of the proposed projects will have had to be rejected or deferred so as to keep the program within the limits of the resources available. Those projects actually included in the plan will have been selected in order of their priority, and this priority will doubtless have been determined according to the value of the project in promoting the program of which the projects are a part.

Resource Allocation

The really big complication for a crime prevention planner will be the allocation of the resources available among the competing subsectors that are his concern. This is, of course, the problem for *all* planners and is no more than a sectoral application of the fundamental economic problem of allocating scarce resources among alternative ends and means.

Logically, it should be a process readily determined by the assigning of priorities and the careful weighing of a country's needs. If a plan has clear guidelines, these should simplify resource allocations. But the term *competing* is used here advisedly, because it would be totally naive and unrealistic to imagine that the subsectors that comprise existing services in crime prevention are passive receivers or that they will not have their own vested interests. Naturally, they will be anxious to attract the funds they need for their own particular projects. Often jobs and job development are at stake when it is a question of the availability of government funds; powerful bureaucratic and political interests will be seeking to pursue their own ends.

Is it better to give the lion's share of crime prevention funds to the improvement of police services, which are, after all, the first line of defense? Or is it more realistic to make sure that those arrested are dealt with by correctional services so very much improved that recidivism is effectively decreased? Should most of the money go to better child care services in the hope of reducing the recruitment of maladjusted or antisocial children to the criminal population? Or would it not be better to develop education in such a way that the socialization process in schools is improved and helps to correct the deficiencies in home care? If there are more deaths on the road because of careless or drunken driving than there are as a result of other criminal activities, should road development and stricter supervision of driving standards be allocated a greater share of the available funds?

These are only a few of the obvious questions for a planner to answer. A natural inclination might be to say that each one of these areas should get its fair share of attention; but this is an escape in words that does not readily apply in practice. The issue for the planner is to decide exactly what that share should be. If there is an equal division of available funds, then nothing new may be achieved. And what is worse, the older unsuccessful methods may be perpetuated unprofitably. If the existing strengths of the ministries or services concerned are reflected faithfully in the fund allocations, this is less a plan than a description of the *status quo*; the opportunity to move in some new direction and to correct imbalances may be lost. On the other hand, new initiatives and planning approaches that alter the established balance or accepted hierarchy of interest will need general acceptance or higher authority if they are to work. They will need power and weight if they are to prevail over rooted interests that have access to authority. The planner will have to come to some conclusions in order to make his allocations of funds, even if the vested interests are powerful in making such decisions. Even when crime is low and institutions can be closed, there may be resistance to changes that mean a loss of jobs or privileges for some. Where crime is high, the demands for more staff and facilities is heard on all sides at once. And the question of whether to concentrate investments for optimal effect or to distribute them over a wider range of services is always likely to be challenged. It would be easier if criminological research had been able to show where the emphasis should be placed, but unfortunately this is not yet the situation. And, as indicated above, the planner will, in the early stages at least, be in some difficulty in weighting objectively the value of his competing projects and programs. After the first plan implementation period, he will at least have evaluations of past efforts to inform his choice. Even if some of these prove to be ambiguous, the situation for decision-making will be clearer than it could have been without consistent evaluation.

Nor should it be imagined that the total amount of money or other available resources for crime prevention will always have been earmarked in advance. The crime prevention sector may have been given a definite allocation; but it is also likely that the crime prevention planner may have to draw up—with the aid of his subsectoral colleagues or any crime prevention planning committee—the best crime prevention plan he can devise and then compete with other sectors for an allocation of the total resources available for a national plan. Where this happens, the likely outcome is that crime prevention will, in the result, get rather less than it asked for; and the specialist planner—with or without his committee or subsectoral colleagues—will need to reshape his crime prevention plan to fit the resources—cutting out those programs or projects with the least priority. Typically, the tendency is to inflate the proposed plan in order to take into account the inevitable cuts. This is usual if not always defensible. But whether a sum is determined in advance as a percentage of the available resources or is arrived at after the paring of a proposed scheme, it is reasonable to assume that it will be less than sufficient to meet all demands and a choice in quantified money terms will have to be made.

Of course, if the country is rich, urbanized, and greatly troubled with crime, it could be that there will be more funds voted for law and order than the existing crime prevention programs can properly use. This is the exceptional case, however. When it does happen, there is an obvious danger of programs and projects being devised simply to use the available resources, and the effects on crime are likely to be doubtful. Solutions cannot be bought if they don't yet exist. In fact, there are few countries with funds sufficiently large to spend in this way. Typically, a country never has enough funds to allow a really effective crime prevention plan to be fully implemented, and the planner has to allocate his scarce resources to obtain an optimal effect.

Plan Implementation and Coordination

It has become customary for planners to distinguish between plan *execution* and plan *implementation*. Briefly, the former means carrying out the specific tasks that the plan has been designed to ensure, e.g., building schools, training more police, adding parole officers, and doing the research specified, while the latter (plan implementation) is used in a wider sense to cover not only the execution but also its preparation, coordination, and control, as well as follow-up, evaluation, and revisions to the plan.

Too often the best plans have been ineffective because inadequate attention was paid to implementation. For instance, the Malaysian Ministry of Welfare Service, in its second plan (Ranchangan Malaysia Kedua 1971-1975), states:

Since all development requires an initial emphasis on increasing physical output there is a tendency to think of development as primarily an economic process and physical reality. It has taken the entire "Development Decade" for planners to realise that an equally important element in national development concerns the response of citizens to Governmental Planning efforts. The assumption, often taken for granted, has been that once the mechanism for development has been established and the plans formulated, the support and enthusiasm of the people will automatically follow. This assumption has been repeatedly proved to be largely unfounded. On the other hand, while planning methods and techniques have been developed to a comparatively high degree of sophistication, the strategies and methods of implementation have not been sufficiently developed and oriented to local conditions. As a result, the formal organisations, structures, and social institutions established for the implementation of plans have been out of gear with, and been unable to capture, the imagination and aspirations of the people and appear unrelated to the real needs of people as conceived by them.

In crime prevention, plan implementation means not merely the work connected with the programs in each of the subsectors, e.g., police, prisons, parole, protection, social services, etc., but providing effectively for regular consultation between these services during and, if possible, prior to the action being undertaken. It implies building into the total plan—and perhaps into each subsectoral program—the machinery needed for coordination and evaluation. It also means effective public relations and community involvement at nearly all stages of an operation. Crime is essentially a community problem that cannot usually be solved by specialist services if these do not have full public support.

Incidentally, experience indicates that there is no more effective coordination than the central control of any additional funds. This encourages the coordination necessary to qualify for the extra funds. It would be idealistic to imagine that personality differences do not intervene in effective coordination; too often, too many persons (including many officials) want the credit, and may even opt out of programs unlikely to reflect credit directly to their own contribution. Too often, the very structures of a government or ministry or a group of Ministries or departments is such that on a day-to-day basis coordination is difficult to ensure, despite a great deal of good-will, persistent exhortation, and any number of regular meetings designed to coordinate. Human nature being what it is, and the power structures of our social organization being what they are, coordination appears to come more easily where it is either enjoined by authority (so that there is a loss of status or the likelihood of penalization from a resistance to coordination) or where it is evinced by the promise of more funds and more departmental development in return for more consideration being given to dovetailing the Ministry's work with that of other Ministries or agencies. This may be the "carrot and stick" approach, but the facts are available from long experience. In Iran, the success over the years of the Plan Organization has owed much to the support of the Shah, whose determination to obtain better results permeated the government structure. In Kenya some years ago, a rivalry between the Ministries of Plan and Agriculture affected development; and in many developed countries rivalries between police and prison departments or between Home and Justice Ministries have been inimical to reasonable coordination. In international spheres, the United Nations Special Fund was able to draw agencies together for cooperation in the implementation of coordinated programs. Examples like this are not difficult to multiply.

It is evident from discussions of the courses already held that the coordination of crime prevention services with more general economic and social development has been one of the prime areas of concern. Thailand has a governmental structure that covers most of the requirements for crime prevention, but coordination is still required at all levels. Afghanistan, the Philippines, Ceylon, Korea, and even Japan faced this problem of adequate coordination for the prevention of crime.

Among the devices to induce coordination, it could be said that wherever it might be possible to make additional funds contingent upon the various crime prevention services getting together to plan and integrate their activities, this could be expected to encourage coordination. It usually provides the incentive to work together. Where it is possible after the event to reward successfully coordinated projects by choosing these same groups of Departments or Ministries for future aid from any additional central funds, this again will help. The services will work together to ensure their own future development by means of future allocations. All of which suggest that the mere pouring out of funds into no more than the established official channels of expenditure on the submission of a variety of new schemes and without special thought given to coordination is very questionable as a method of getting results. More hope of success flows from the attempt to design coordinated programs for special financing.

Task forces, special commissions, and interdepartmental committees have been set up in some countries to cut across the traditional subsectoral boundaries. These are valuable when they (a) have the power and funds to act and maintain a long-term program of action, and (b) when they are sufficiently short term to outline the issues and leave the established services to deal with them. Task forces, working parties, and commissions of this kind appear to be correspondingly less valuable when they absorb scarce resources merely to dramatize what is already known, when they develop bureaucracies of their own that become self-perpetuating, and when they last too long to have a good impulse effect or too short to take some responsibility for the action required to remedy the problem. And in any event, bodies such as these are effective as a rule only according to the knowledge, skill, and ability of the executive personnel that serve them. However prestigious and influential the membership, an efficient secretariat is usually required to carry their decisions into effect.

Probably no organization has yet completely solved the problem of efficient and satisfactory coordination of its work. The bigger the establishment and more rigid the bureaucracy, the more important such coordination becomes—but by the same token, the more difficult it is to achieve. In plan implementation the need to coordinate action is as obvious as it is problematic. The example has already been given of one country in which the Plan Organization actually took over from the Ministries the implementation of the national plan so as to ensure effective execution. This is hardly to be recommended, if only because the Ministries need to be brought back into the picture sooner or later. In the case quoted, the responsibility of the Ministries for the implementation of plans was restored within a few years and is now again unquestioned. The action of the Plan Organization, although effective, was deeply resented by the Ministries, who soon took up the struggle to regain control. In any case, it cannot be claimed that even with such drastic measures, and even with the Plan Organization assuming full responsibility for implementation, the coordination was everything that might have been desired.

The control of plan implementation is a subject that has received less attention in the literature than it really deserves. But accountability at all levels, the monitoring of funds, the checking of progress on specific projects, and the making of necessary readjustments in the light of results or events are all important areas of control. One real problem derives from an overcontrolled implementation that places the monitoring in the hands of administrators who know little or nothing about the substantive plans and projects but are expert in devising managerial formulae, progress report schedules, and all kinds of vouchers, returns, and statements to control funds, complicate procedures, "rationalize" purchases, and time schedules and periodic reports in such myriad and infinite detail that they eventually clutter the machinery of implementation with a great mass of paper. The extra machinery for the efficient handling of the procedures becomes a technique unrelated to the field work, but which it ultimately tends to dominate with all the formal requirements and routines of a ponderous bureaucracy. Some growth of administration is both necessary and useful to obtain efficiency of implementation and to ensure the procedures and controls that will reduce waste. But it is a growth that inclines to cancerous proportions if it is not carefully controlled and streamlined from time to time. It can absorb scarce resources and make it necessary to remove a mountain to get to a molehill. The letter of the regulations rather than the spirit begins to prevail, and the essential project or program can become administratively choked, if the objectives are not kept firmly in sight and the procedures kept to an efficient minimum.

The balance is never easy to strike; but it would seem desirable to place the control of a plan in a decentralized pattern that devolves to the professional involved as much freedom to operate and report as it is possible to give—consistent of course with the availability of adequate reports for the appropriate committees. One device is to place the administrators *under* the control of the responsible professional officers, so as to ensure that the necessary minimum of administrative work gets done without cluttering the field work.

Finally, in crime prevention planning the involvement of the public should be examined at its lowest levels as well as the highest levels. This has always been the real answer to crime. The ancient hue and cry depended upon the public being used effectively—as did the sheriff's posse. The older forms of compurgation and collective responsibility, though abused by unpopular regimes, have a legitimate use in developing a neighborhood involvement in crime prevention. In the past, the West has relied far too much upon better communications and improved technical services or higher proportions of specialized manpower to prevent crime. This leaves the local citizen too dependent upon official action and too uninvolved for his own adequate protection. It is interesting in this respect to observe that public participation in crime control often means to the professional police or correctional officer the mobilizing of the public to implement official action. But in a true democracy it could well mean the professional staff serving the purposes decided for them by public committees and responding more effectively to felt public needs.

Evaluation

On follow-up and evaluation a great deal has been written already. Obviously it is essential to be able to evaluate the work done in crime prevention in terms of less crime, less serious crime, less recidivism, or more effective and efficient methods for dealing with crime. But it is evident that much of the criteria for measurement in this field will be lacking for some time to come.

In general the evaluation of anything can be reduced to three main categories of criteria. There is an overlap between them but each is a distinct approach.

Category 1

Has value been obtained for the money spent and the resources invested? This is, at first sight, a specifically economic standard or measure. In fact it is much more, for the concept of "value" is more than economic. Projects with little or no economic benefits can be seen as valuable by governments in that they have advanced, or contributed to, official policy. This is especially true of social projects. A rehabilitation service for the disabled, for instance, may have succeeded even if it could show no economic return—simply because it served the humanitarian ends for which it was introduced. A rehabilitation or reintegration service for ex-prisoners could have similar noneconomic justification. However, it may be possible to show substantial economic returns as well if the perspectives are widened. The returns to the individual and his family traced into a succeeding generation could be significant. The effect of the scheme on the hopes and aspirations of people still in custody might be added, if this means a greater commitment to work in these institutions and is less expensive in terms of purely custodial staff. The benefits to persons employed to run the rehabilitation or reintegration schemes might also be added—not only their earnings distributed as benefits to their families carried again to a future generation, but also the value of their training that enables them to be used in other such schemes or even in other types of employment. Finally the material benefit to society must be added by showing the amounts that might have been lost or the damage that would have been done if these persons had returned to their earlier forms of crime. The opportunity costs (of using staff in this way, which could have been engaged in productive work had they not been employed at the center) would of course have to be charged against these benefits.

Category 2

Value for whom? Once the purely accounting practices are overreached, it becomes necessary to include here the political return to the government in power. If a project not showing a monetary benefit contributes nevertheless to a satisfied populace, ensures votes, and political support, there may be substantial monetary value in the long run. A welfare scheme may seem wasteful of resources, but if it maintains in power a government that is able to carry a peaceful country to higher levels of development without revolution or disorder, it has a calculable material benefit. The investment is showing returns in all other sectors of the economy, even though the link might not be so easy to establish. Similarly, an investment in allowances for the families of prisoners may have a spin-off that prevents crime in the next generation.

Secondly, one should not overlook the value to the bureaucracy providing the service. There is an employment effect, a growth of the establishment, and an increase in its influence on the policy-makers. Once again, these have to be discounted against opportunity costs, but if the country has an unemployment problem, this may not be high. Also there is the value to the staff employed and their families.

Thirdly, there is the value, monetary and nonmonetary, to the recipients of aid. In crime prevention if this means diverting them from dangerous or predatory activities, then the opportunity costs are small.

Finally there is the benefit to the general public, which is kept at a higher level of safety and permitted to go about its productive work more effectively. The value in reducing insurance premiums and, thereby, the prices of commodities also deserves more consideration than it has received in the past.

Category 3

This consists of more specific criteria for the success of a project. There are five of these that can be applied to any project or program.

1. **Its Effectiveness.** Did it achieve its declared goals—or did it achieve the objectives that are imputable by its nature?

2. **Its Significance.** Even if it did achieve its goals, so what? What was its significance for the country, for the region, or for those involved? This needs to be investigated politically, socially and economically.

3. **Its Efficiency.** What were its costs and returns? This is considered in more detail below.

4. **Its Compliance.** To what extent did it adhere to the original formulation? Did it achieve its objectives by the means provided for—or by other unexpected procedures.

5. **Its Unanticipated Effects and Byproducts.** How much of the achievement was unexpected? What were the side effects that had not been foreseen in the original formulation?

It should be noted that in any given case there is no reason why the answers to these questions should coincide. An efficient project showing a multiplier effect for a small investment may have achieved this result by a departure from the terms originally formulated—or its returns might not be in tune with its original objectives, so that it might not qualify for being called effective. Nor would the evaluation within the three broad categories support each other; if one applies the criteria of Category 2, then there could be success even if all the questions of Category 3 had to be answered negatively.

A clear statement of objectives is obviously a *sine qua non* for evaluation. But, equally obviously, objectives widen out in ripples from a given center. Thus, the limited objectives of a housing, health, welfare, police, court, or prisons project might well be achieved without contributing in any way to the wider sectoral objectives. Courts might be made more efficient without the incidence of a particular form of crime being reduced. Police improvements might increase rather than decrease the numbers of cases to be handled. Public safety might be reduced by the death penalty, if this meant greater desperation in those killers on the run who sought to escape death at all costs. Conversely, sectoral objectives are sometimes achievable at the expense of the national plan, e.g., if the success of a crime prevention set of programs could only be achieved by diversing resources from more productive uses. This is more obvious where, for example, the success of a health project increases populations and thereby the pressures on local incomes. Evaluation must therefore examine the objectives from several points of view.

Again, there are inevitably a number of imponderable elements in any study of a project or program. An evaluator has necessarily to speculate on what might have happened if the program or project had never been undertaken. He has to ask whether the same or better results might have been obtained by some other approach, by other methods, or by a different kind of project altogether. Above all, he has to ask whether it might not have been preferable to avoid all official intervention, e.g., by not enacting the crime creating laws in the first place.

The attempt in raising all these difficulties attached to an evaluation is indeed to induce a sense of humility in evaluators rather than to cast doubt on the process of evaluation itself. With all its present shortcomings—especially when applied to crime prevention work—evaluation is still a most valuable way of improving introspection and a healthy attitude of self-questioning. Even if it leaves many issues open or only subsequently answered, evaluation makes a vital contribution to the efficiency of future work. It promotes clearer thinking, lays bare some of the underlying assumptions, and uncovers differences of interpretation, which could have been clogging or misrepresenting an operation. It has the value of broadening the horizons of those engaged in the work and exposing wider relationships and implications that are not always self-evident. Helping those involved in the work to take a broader view of what they are doing casts doubt on a good deal of misplaced zeal for narrow sectoral or project objectives.

Above all it serves to expose the great mistake of valuing what is quantifiable instead of seeking to quantify what is valuable.

There are some real difficulties in applying evaluation to crime prevention. Crime statistics are too vulnerable to adjustment or too sensitive to change in administrative procedure to be infallible guides to the amount of crime or its degree of seriousness. Victimology surveys, with which official statistics should be combined, are still crude. The levels of security or satisfaction in the community are practically impossible to measure, except in some public opinion poll designed for a limited purpose. And the testing of reintegration or prevention by certain techniques of correction and control still requires refinement. If all the variables in number of police, police policy, sentencing, correctional practices, and criminogenic environment could be held constant, one year's returns might be comparable with another—but the variables cannot be so held. And even evaluation by comparison means some assumptions about the constancy of factors.

Nevertheless, if crime prevention planning means anything at all, it means setting both goals and bench marks, however many shortcomings these may have. And correspondingly, evaluation must be based upon some kind of assessment of the progress made in realizing these goals. Crime figures will have to be used, and it might not be such a farfetched idea to arrange a periodic public opinion poll as a monitor of progress—if it can be independently contrived. In any case, it is to be hoped that with the passage of time more work will be done on the use of social indicators[c] and on techniques of evaluation that give more of a basis for the development of follow-up and evaluation in crime prevention.

Plan implementation and the decision-making connected with budgeting have been the subject of study and experimentation that have resulted in several devices for the rationalization and allocation of resources and approaches to evaluation. Not all are applicable to crime prevention, though attempts have been, and are being, made to adapt them. One or two are provided here, only to show method. Their precise adaption to crime prevention situations would require a further study of prepared cases or projects.

Cost-Benefit Analysis

Cost-benefit analysis is self-descriptive, i.e., based upon a comparison of possible, probable, and certain *benefits* of a project or program with the foreseeable *costs* or outlays. It is a technique that can be useful in deciding whether a project or program ought to have been undertaken or ought to be undertaken. Often a

[c]Social indicators are still being developed for planning purposes, but already there are useful guides to progress in figures for mortality rates (especially infant mortality), morbidity rates, and educational levels.

project will not be undertaken if the benefits are not expected to exceed costs, and cost-benefit analysis has been used to show the value in the long term of some large investment over the next few years. Cost-benefit provides a method of selecting between a number of different ways of achievement or effecting an objective. First, there is usually established a so-called universe of candidate projects, i.e., a range of competing schemes. Rough judgment reduces these to a short list, which is then subjected to feasibility studies and cost-benefit (or yield-cost) analysis to make selection easier. This is the forward looking use of the method. Its backward looking application is its application in determining the ratio between what a project has in fact achieved and the amount of resources invested.

It is easier to do this for economic projects. However, for social schemes all kinds of criteria have to be used to quantify the benefits. The effects, or possible effects, on future earnings of individuals trained, for example, have been used (the actual increases in earning power being calculated for several years ahead to show the expected return). In this way, the costs of a course or a health scheme have been offset against the added income to be expected by the individual. For economic projects the classic example, often used in the textbooks, is the anlaysis that was made of the costs and benefits of the London Underground System before it was built. Here the costs were so high as to be a real deterrant, but when the benefits of a swifter transport system were worked out for the traveling public, not only for the first decade but over a long period of years, and the probable effects of this costed for the population as a whole, the costs seemed not only less, but in perspective, both reasonable and justifiable.

Obviously, cost-benefit analysis is of most use where there is the prospect of ready quantification and conversion into money terms. Then the streams of income and expenditure on a project can be phased over a number of years, interest rates can be discounted, depreciation allowed for, and the various factors weighted. However, social values are not so easily quantified and, even when quantified, they often cannot be appraised in money terms despite the efforts that have been, and are being, made to give monetary expression to social values. Actual money spent on solving problems, its significance in the saving of work hours, or the social costs involved in taking no action have all been used and are all legitimate in the attempt to quantify the largely unquantifiable. But it would be a mistake to believe that all social imperatives or social needs readily lend themselves to the kind of mathematical shorthand that is so useful with trade figures, output calculations, and labor statistics.

Indeed it cannot be assumed necessarily that cost-benefit analysis can resolve some of the main priority issues, for a great deal depends upon the time factor and the relationship between cost and other national objectives. This century has seen many countries for political or ideological reasons take the path of self-denial and prefer the more unprofitable allocations of resources to those projects that would, on the basis of simple cost-benefit analysis, have low ratings. At election time cost-benefit considerations may be deferred to ensure support for programs of wider appeal.

The planner might say that all these are extraneous considerations that do not concern him—and that his task is simply to show the cost and benefit implications of certain decisions. The fact is, however, that these other considerations may well have direct economic implications when the time factor is included—for cost-benefit analysis always depends upon the time spread. Who can say, for example, that some countries now politically important after long periods of self-denial and a refusal to follow the most economically profitable policies might not benefit far more economically in the long term? Who can be sure that a country choosing to spend on defense to preserve independence is not more likely to be economically wiser in the long run? And, if a really long period is under consideration, then the cost-benefit factor might be transformed. Imagine the result of a cost-benefit analysis prepared for the Pharoahs of Egypt on the building of the Pyramids or for the Shoguns of Japan on temple building. The results would certainly have been negative, at least, until the really long term was taken into account. If the economists (or their equivalent) of those days could have looked forward to improvements in modern travel and the great earning potential of tourism, they would not have needed to justify these buildings in terms of the after life or spiritual imperatives—they would have been able to show economic returns for the country vastly exceeding any outlay of funds.

Therefore, whenever cost-benefit analyses are under consideration, it is important to present them in varying contexts. Just as the London Underground could be justified by widening the factors to be weighted and calculated over a number of years, so many other projects look different when viewed within a longer time perspective. The railway linking Lusaka with Dar es Salaam in Africa was conceived for political reasons—to emancipate Zambia from its dependence on the railway links to the south, i.e., through Rhodesia and South Africa. On any calculable basis of foreseeable costs and benefits it might not have been possible to justify it economically; but once built—even if it operated at an economic loss—its benefits in terms of independence for Zambia justified it. Moreover, in the years ahead it will doubtless show economic gains outweighing costs.

Normally, planning will be concerned with periods of 5 or 10 years and with costs and advantages to the present or succeeding generations. This is both practical and reasonable, and the significance of cost-benefit analysis cannot be overestimated. The technique is limited, however, even in the economic sense, when longer time spans or wider ranges of national interests have to be incorporated in the decision-making; it is even more limited where qualities are of prime concern.

This should be no excuse for failure to systematically present the items in a plan that are not quantifiable. However, where figures can be given, they should be used. Probably any improvement in this is better than the earlier very casual treatment of crime, pollution, and other social costs, which have been neglected in planning so very often in the past. However, the value of cost-benefit analysis for social projects has a usefulness that will decline to the extent that nonmonetary benefits constitute a share of the total expectations. The larger the nonmonetary share, the more questionable the application of a cost-benefit technique.

The application of the cost-benefit analysis to criminal justice has occurred mainly in the U.S.A. Landers offered a model building approach in 1971, assuming:

1. The prosecutor maximizes the expected number of convictions weighted by their sentences subject to a budget constraint.
2. The defendant maximizes the expected utility of his endorsements in various states of the world.[2]

He sought to postulate and test a number of hypotheses. He tried, for instance, to demonstrate by this method that the relationship between bail and trials in some courts was due to cost rather than wealth differentials. The demands for trial were negatively correlated to the delays that occurred in trials and positively correlated to the delays that occurred in settlement. Also, measuring conviction probabilities by the proportion of defendants imprisoned, he sought to indicate that the likelihood of a conviction was greater for those not released on bail in the courts he studied. This is readily challengeable by widening the facts taken into account or challenging the assumptions, but the method could doubtless be refined and validated within its own context.

Another way of approaching cost-benefit for social programs is via a specialized rating system, i.e., setting up a rating scale based upon reliable appraisals by the people who are being served by the programs. This is a nonmonetary device with its own limitations, but it could be more widely used than it has been thus far. Vanecko used the rating of selected persons in fifty U.S. cities to test the increase of services produced by Community Action Programs, comparing those that emphasized public participation with those that concentrated more on the better coordination of existing services. He concluded that where citizen participation was stressed more services were produced.[3]

Cost Effectiveness

This amounts to a restricted version of cost-benefit analysis. It begins with a specified objective and an account of the costs involved in providing for a number of alternative programs or projects for attaining the objectives. Here the objective need not be monetarily quantifiable, the aim could be to achieve a decrease in the infant mortality rate or an increase in literacy. In cost effectiveness there is a compromise between the effectiveness of different possible programs or projects. However, it will be clear that the less comparable the objectives or ends, the more restricted becomes the range of systematic or rational choice demanded by this and other kinds of planning techniques. Rather than generalize, it is perhaps more instructive to take illustration's of cost-benefit/cost effectiveness analysis.

Example from Outside the Criminal Justice System

In 1964 Michael E. Borus published, as part of a doctoral thesis, a study of "The Economic Effectiveness of Retraining the Unemployed."[4] The purpose of the study was to weigh the benefits and costs of retraining programs to determine if they were a sound investment for (a) the individual worker, (b) the government, or (c) the economy.

The relevance for crime prevention—and especially the correctional services—is fairly immediate, since very often benefits and costs can be distributed between the community and the individual as well as the criminal justice services.

The objectives of this retraining program study were:

1. To determine the economic benefits derived from retraining, by the individual worker, the government, and the economy.
2. To determine the economic costs of the retraining to the individual worker, the government, and the economy.
3. To compare these economic benefits and costs with a view to determining the value of retraining as an investment opportunity for the individual worker, the government, and the economy.

To obtain this information a sample of 373 workers (312 men and 61 women) were selected and classified into six groups:

1. Workers who utilized retraining.
2. Workers who completed retraining but did not use it.
3. Workers who withdrew from retraining without employment.
4. Workers who withdrew from retraining for employment.
5. Workers who refused retraining for employment.
6. Workers who refused retraining without employment.

In a rather subtle interfacing of the information obtained from these groups, the workers in 2, 3, and 6 were used as a control group for comparison with the others. The research questions were divided into those under benefits, those under costs, and those connected with the comparison.

A. Benefits. Research questions pertaining to the individual:

1. Do the employment records of the workers who utilized the retraining show significant gross improvements when compared with the employment records of the control group? (The application of this to offenders trained or supervised and others not trained or supervised will be noted.)
2. Are there factors that reduce the gross benefits in income?
3. What is the expected duration of these benefits?
4. To what extent would the worker have enjoyed these benefits, had he not been retrained?
5. What time horizon does the worker use to calculate the benefits?
6. What is the probability that a given worker will use the retraining?
7. What are the expected benefits of retraining for an average worker based upon the experience of the workers in the sample?

Research questions pertaining to the government and total economy:

1. Have the retrained workers displaced other workers, or have they induced other reductions in production or employment that might offset the individual benefits?
2. What effects does the existence of less than full employment have on the aggregate benefits?
3. What is the expected duration of the aggregate benefits?
4. What are the expected benefits to the government per worker who enters retraining, based upon the experience of the workers in the sample?
5. What are the expected benefits to the total economy per worker who enters retraining, based on the experience of the workers in the sample?

B. Costs. Research questions considered:

1. What are the approximate costs of retraining to the workers, based on the experience of the sample?
2. What are the average government costs per worker who enters retraining, based on the experience of the sample?
3. What are the average costs to the total economy of each worker who enters retraining, based on the experience of the sample?
4. What would be the effect of an alternative proposal on aggregate costs?

C. Comparison. Research questions considered:

1. Do the benefits when weighed against the costs justify the retraining program as an investment for the individual?
2. Do the benefits when weighed against the costs justify the retraining program as an investment for the government?

3. Do the benefits when weighed against the costs justify the retraining program as an investment for the total economy?
4. How would the benefit-cost ratio change if the alternative proposals were adopted?

Finally, the study asked whether alternative sponsors for the program would be more profitable, e.g., if costs were to be borne by the individual or the private sector, and what effect this might have upon the number and composition of the workers to be retrained.

The results of seeking the specific answers to these questions were as follows.

A. Individual Benefits. These were held to derive from (a) any increase in the worker's disposable income and (b) any decrease in his periods of unemployment, where both of these could be ascribed to his retraining.

By linear multiple regression techniques that take account of the different demographic characteristics of the retrainees and those in the control groups, it was found that workers who were retrained and used the retraining earned on the average $7.44 more per week than did workers who completed but did not use the retraining, $8.83 more per week than did workers who refused retraining without employment, and $15.06 more per week than workers who withdrew from retraining without employment.

When quarterly rather than weekly earnings were compared, the advantages of those using their retraining were increased over the other groups.

However, it was found that the real benefits to the workers using their retraining flowed more from the reduction in the periods of unemployment than from any differences in the hourly wage rates. Those who used their retraining decreased their periods of unemployment by about 10 percent.

On the average the individual who used his retraining increased his first year's income by about $500 and reduced his annual unemployment by about 5 weeks in the year.

This was not all gain, however. Against these benefits it was necessary to offset the worker's losses from increased taxation payments and the discontinuance of unemployment pay. Thus, on the average a worker using his retraining added $500 to his yearly income and lost about $100 of this in additional taxes and social security payments—and he lost another $100 by the discontinuation of his unemployment pay.

Nor could all the increased benefits be attributed precisely to the retraining. It had to be acknowledged that some of the workers might well have been placed in the same occupations even if they had not been retrained. Without going into all the details, it emerged that this could have been true of about 20 percent of the total of those using their retraining. As, however, there were similar percentages of workers in the control groups who had been placed in retraining related employment, it was decided, for the purposes of the study, that this kind of discounting cancelled itself out and did not detract from the benefits.

It must be remembered that one is dealing here with the first year after retraining. When longer-time periods have to be taken into account, the possibility of advantages being offset by later events—and especially by the mobility of the labor force—has to be recognized. Some 24 percent of the workers in the sample who were originally placed in retraining—related occupations—left for other jobs within one year of completing the course. Of this group about one fourth moved, again to occupations that still made some use of the retraining; another 18 percent moved to unrelated jobs. If this rate of mobility were to be projected 5 years after completion of the course, only 37 percent of the workers who initially used their training would still be using it—and in 10 years this would be reduced to only 14 percent. The study referred to other surveys of labor mobility to show that this was a rather exaggerated projection, and eventually it took a rather more reassuring rate of the forward use in the training received. The possibility of some workers moving out of retraining-related occupations and then moving back into training-related jobs had also to be considered.

It seemed, therefore, that in the first year the benefit to workers using their retraining was some $300, but 19 percent of these workers would have been in the same occupations even if they had not retrained. In subsequent years 18 percent per year could be expected to move into jobs not related to the retraining, and a further discount was made to take account of the individual worker's own time preference in calculating his advantages from taking the course. Moreover, since 20.3 percent of all those who took the course withdrew, and 16 percent on graduation found jobs that did not use the training, it seemed that the average worker in the sample who took the course had only a 0.67 probability of deriving the benefits referred to here.

Benefits to the Economy and the Government. The stated objectives of the authorities in sponsoring the retraining of the unemployed were:

1. To increase the nation's output.
2. To reduce the aggregate level of unemployment.
3. To reduce the costs of unemployment and public assistance.
4. To reduce the burdens of unemployment for specific groups of unemployed.

The first two of these are benefits for the economy. They also serve to delineate the economic benefits for the government, in that a rise in GNP as a result of retraining increases tax revenues and also any reduction in the aggregate rate of unemployment reduces government expenditure for unemployment benefits. Thus, the third objective, which is not a benefit for the economy since it reduces transfer payments rather than real costs, is a benefit for the government. The fourth of these objectives is not a benefit to either the government or the economy since it is basically a matter of income redistribution—but indirectly it affects economic benefits by affecting the number and percentage of workers who are placed.

Under certain conditions the benefits for the individual discussed above are also benefits for the economy. These conditions are:

1. That retrainees do not displace other workers in the retraining occupations. This would merely shift the unemployment without reducing it.
2. That there are no other workers in the unemployed labor force who are able and willing, without entering the retraining courses, to fill the available job openings and who are therefore being displaced by the retrainees.
3. That, in the absence of retraining, the labor force would not adapt to the labor shortages in the retraining occupations, while the benefits still accrue to the individual.
4. That there exist no unemployed workers who will fill the jobs left by the retrained workers when they enter the retraining occupations.
5. That there are no secondary effects from the increase in income that results from the retraining.
6. That the social rate of time preference is equal to that of the individual.

The study could not find sufficient direct evidence to answer all these points conclusively and had to rely upon circumstantial evidence. It was supposed that the Act authorizing the retraining was based upon fairly accurate estimations of labor shortage by the State Employment Services and, therefore, that workers were not being displaced. The fact that the courses were continuing was also taken as an indication that workers were not being displaced by the flow of retrainees. If displacement had been occurring, this would have become evident to the State Employment Services and the course would have been changed accordingly. This had not happened. Similarly, had there been available persons able to fill the jobs without retraining, it would have been unlikely that the employers would have kept these places vacant for so long. It was significant that 84 percent of the sample completing the courses had been placed in jobs needing the skills in which they were trained. In addition, many of the remaining 16 percent were offered jobs they did not accept.

As regards the possible adaption of the labor force to the shortages, it was possible to predict such adjustments. Nevertheless, even with the retraining programs the labor shortages continued to exist 3 years after the courses were begun, which would seem to indicate that adaptation was slow if, indeed, it was taking place at all.

On the fourth condition, it is clear that the extent to which retraining benefits the economy depends on how well the economy is using its labor resources. If retraining the labor force merely upgrades individual workers without affecting aggregate employment, the effect of the retraining is to increase the GNP only by the increment in the worker's output over their expected output in the absence of retraining. However, if aggregate employment is increased by retraining, either by placing an unemployed worker in an occupation that has an inadequate supply of labor or by placing an employed unskilled worker in a semiskilled occupation and an unemployed worker in the newly created unskilled vacancy, then the GNP will increase by the entire output of the retrained worker.

For the workers in the sample, this latter case seemed to apply. For example 70 percent of the workers who used the retraining were unemployed at the time they took the aptitude test for the retraining course. The majority of another 23 percent were employed in unskilled jobs, which could easily be filled from among the unemployed. Thus, the average sampled worker's gross annual contribution to GNP was not the $500 in wage income that he received but $4,358.70, i.e., the total of his output or the gross addition to production that resulted from the retraining.

Moreover, since the retraining took place in a less than fully employed economy, the increase in production and income could be expected to have a multiplier effect, increasing the benefits in real terms to the economy and to the government. A multiplier of 2 was adopted for the purpose of the study.

B. Costs. The cost of retraining had to be calculated on a marginal or "with or without" basis as had been done with benefits. Only the additional costs that would not have been incurred in the absence of the retraining program were considered. For the individual the costs of retraining were any additional expenses that he had to incur to take part in the program and any reduction in income during the course that resulted from his taking part in it. Similarly, the costs for the government included only the variable costs of the State Employment Services and the vocational schools, since the high fixed costs for buildings would exist even in the absence of the retraining program. The Act providing for this particular retraining scheme explicitly forbad the building of new premises for the courses. Finally, the costs of retraining for the economy include any additional government expenditures on real goods and services that are necessary to operate the program and any loss in aggregate production that takes place during the course as a result of the reduced output of staff or retrainees.

For this study the government costs were calculated by taking the work hours per trainee spent by the State Employment Services on initial counselling, testing, issuing nominations, responding to these, and keeping records. This worked out at 15.44 hours per trainee, i.e., some $56.39 per trainee. Instructors' costs, tool crib attendants, and custodial staff ran to $17.06 per week for each of the workers in the sample who entered training. To this administrative costs were added at a rate of $56.20 per trainee, and there was a further $31.66 average weekly cost per trainee for a training allowance—this being the difference between the total training allowance and the amount of unemployment pay that a trainee would have otherwise received.

C. Comparison. Costs were outweighed by the benefits not only to the individual but to the government and to the economy. In the U.S. economy at the time with less than full employment, there were marked external effects resulting from the retraining. This was demonstrated by the fact that the benefit-cost ratios of the government and the economy were greater than the individuals. It was decided to recommend, on the evidence, that as many workers as possible be retrained for occupations that had labor shortages because the net returns from retraining were so great.

On the question of whether the costs should be borne by the individual or the private sector rather than the government, the study recommended the status quo. This was because the return to the government and the economy was demonstrably greater than to industry or to the individual.

It is not suggested that the model provided by this cost-benefit study of a retraining program is transferable in kind to crime prevention projects, but the approach will be suggestive to those looking for ways of tackling the problem of evaluation programs and projects in crime prevention. There is an overlap in the considerations applying to both retraining and rehabilitation, and some of the complications of adequate measurement are well revealed.

Examples of Frustrated Cost Effectiveness Analysis
Within the Criminal Justice System

In January 1975, Gail S. Monkman, the Assistant Project Director of the Correctional Economics Center of the American Bar Association, published a "Cost Analysis of Community Correctional Centers: A Case Study: Indiana." This studied a Community Corrections Center then being planned in Indiana, which was one of the programs intended locally to:

1. Provide adequate supervision of persons awaiting trial who qualify for release on their own recognizance, supervised release, cash bail, or alcohol or drug detoxification.
2. Provide adequate detention of persons awaiting trial who do not so qualify for release.
3. Provide adequate diagnosis and evaluation of adjudicated offenders awaiting sentencing.
4. Reduce by 10 percent the recidivism rate of offenders normally committed to county jails and state correctional institutions by providing adequate correctional programs and residential services at the local level.

5. Reduce by 10 percent the recidivism rate of offenders returning to the area on parole, prerelease, and work-study release by providing adequate correctional programs and residential services at the local level.
6. Reduce by 20 percent the amount of restitution made to victims of property crimes.

These objectives were obviously inspired to no small extent by the report of the National Advisory Committee on Criminal Justice Standards and Goals. This was a committee financed by the Law Enforcement Assistance Administration.[d] The section of its report on corrections stressed the need for community solutions to the problems of correctional services, and it obviously affected State Correctional Services, which were also looking to LEAA for finance. However, Indiana had been looking in this community direction long before the report. For example, Indiana's Public Law 154, enacted in 1971, provided for the establishment of Regional Community Corrections Centers, and Indiana's comprehensive law enforcement plan (also subsidized by LEAA) had included proposals for the Department of Corrections to diversify its management of adjudicated offenders through Community Correctional Centers and programs, declaring that at least one-third of penal institutions' commitments could instead be returned to the community for treatment.

The analysis of the newly developed institution by the Correctional Economics Center concentrated on its pretrial functions, its diagnostic and posttrial functions, and on the projected savings in costs that had doubtless attracted considerable support for the project from legislators and administrators as well as specialists in this field.

The personnel budget proposed for operating the new center for the period July 1975 to June 1976 is shown in Table 3-1. It was observed that this budget was being revised upwards, the most recent change involving medical staff. The CEC (Correctional Economic Center) observed that insofar as pretrial functions were concerned the report had stated that "all persons suitable for pretrial release of some kind will have been screened out and the facility will initially accommodate 120 to 150 persons; yet (the CEC commented) the maximum level of 150 now provided for by this new Community Corrections Center (CCC) actually exceeds the 138 places now occupied by the 135 pretrial detainees *now held* on a daily population basis in a high-security atmosphere." The implication of the building program appeared to be, therefore, that: "no dramatic changes in . . . existing pretrial, release programs which are now basically for misdemeanants with a small pilot extension into selected property crime follows." Thus, it appeared that intentions measured against provisions showed some disparity.

Again the estimated construction costs of the CCC were to be $2,400,000, with annual operating costs of $211,200 for correctional personnel and benefits, plus an approximate prorated cost of $142,000 for administration, medical, and food services. However, it was also discovered that the largest jail (in Allen

[d]See account of LEAA below.

Table 3-1
Indiana Community Corrections Center Personnel Budget for Fiscal 1975-1976

Personnel:		
Administrative		
(1) Superintendent	US$20,000	
(1) Business Manager	12,000	
(1) Research and Training	12,000	
(3) Clerical	18,000	62,000
Pretrial Detention:		
(1) Supervisor	12,000	
(13) Correctional Officers	180,000	192,000
Posttrial Corrections:		
(1) Supervisor	12,000	
(10) Program Managers	100,000	
(20) Unit Managers	180,000	
(3) Clerical	18,000	310,000
Clerical Diagnosis and Evaluation:		
(1) Supervisor	12,000	
(2) Diagnosticians	20,000	
(2) Clerical	12,000	44,000
Medical:		
(½) Physician	10,000	
(4) Nurses	40,000	50,000
Food Services:		
(1) Dietician	10,000	
(2) Cooks	12,000	22,000
10 Percent Insurance, Retirement, and FICA		68,000
Total Personnel Costs		948,000

County) and other regional jails were to continue to operate temporary or overnight lockups. The CEC concluded, therefore, that:

Based simply on costs, it is difficult to determine what 'savings' will occur through this facility. Except for the enrichment of the detention stay, there are no new release plans, no jails are closing, and there is no indication that the average stay for persons awaiting trial will drop from its current 160-180 days.

Of course, as the CEC appreciated, the question of reducing average stay depended not on new correctional facilities alone but also on the decisions made by the police and courts, which usually governed the correctional intake.

CEC drew a comparison between the new CC Center, as proposed and costed, and the pretrial program operating at the time in Des Moines, Iowa, i.e., the Polk County community based corrections program that had been initiated 8 years before and later incorporated residential corrections.[5]

The CEC pointed out that the Des Moines program, based upon the principles of keeping as many people as possible in the community, had been successful. In 1972, 1022 defendants were released through the pretrial program. Of these, over 98 percent appeared for trial, which compared favorably with the existing local bail program. Expenditures in the Des Moines project were primarily for personnel and totalled $54,000 in 1972, i.e., $52 per client released. Other programs, such as supervised pretrial release, had higher per capita costs of $701 per client (i.e., $155,000 for 221 clients in 1972). Yet the sum of these program costs at Des Moines was, said the CEC, less than that which Indiana was prepared to allocate simply as personnel costs for the operation of one secure, pretrial detention facility. The CEC stated:

This is not to imply that pretrial release is appropriate for all individuals, but rather that the plan for the new CC Center might not really be changing or modifying any aspect of the 'front end' of the system and yet appeared to be committing the area to a substantial capital investment—results of which, if correctly analyzed, would no doubt have proved unintended and been of concern to the very officials who developed the plan.

Still commending the Des Moines project, which provided Indiana with a comparison, the CEC explained that the Des Moines scheme had demonstrated the "feasibility of releasing high-risk offenders not normally considered suitable for release." Criteria for release in Des Moines applied to all regardless of the alleged offense. The dollar savings to the community as a result of the Des Moines program:

. . . were substantial in the form of reduced jail costs, welfare payments, and foregone earnings, etc. More important, however, are the *human* savings (which can be costed out) that resulted from the Polk County program. Of the 25,681 jail days which were saved through liberalized pretrial release programs, 13,006 of these days were for individuals found not guilty. Additionally program participants generally received fewer convictions and shorter sentences.

Against this background the CEC concluded that the proposed CC Center in Indiana was not cost effective:

It would seem then that . . . the decision to build another secure detention facility would not basically change the system, but rather will solidify detention as approach and solution without significant cost savings.

On the diagnostic and posttrial function of the proposed CC Center for Indiana, the CEC criticized the lack of specificity as to how the CC Center residents would actually use the community services that were to be bought. There was a lack of clarity in the types of services that inmates were to use. While the existing community services (i.e., social amenities, employment, and welfare services) were described, the questions of eligibility and degrees of eligibility were not detailed with the kind of precision that would facilitate comparisons of costs and benefits. Nor had the levels of community receptivity to the plans for inmates been researched. Even eligibility for admission to the CCC was not as clear as it could have been. There was no itemization of the community services that were likely to be required by different inmates. While diagnosis might help to decide this, it was *post facto* rather than planned for. The analysis of the CEC did not add, as it might well have done, that in practice the entire process of diagnosis, as this relates to corrections, is being challenged; so that the linkage between this and community services must be clarified at all stages.

The planning for the proposed CCC had postulated savings, as has been shown. These were expressed in the numbers of inmate days "saved" rather than in dollars. The posttrial correctional part of the CCC would be expected to "handle" 36,500 residential days (which would otherwise have been spent in state institutions and jails), and the concept of averted costs (i.e., by transferring people from existing institutions and dealing with them by alternative programs) had been used. The CEC was able to demonstrate that there were many institutional operating costs that were fixed and could not be averted by a new CCC unless it could replace the older facility. Moreover, real savings in the criminal justice sector are achieved by diverting people from the procedures of arrest, prosecution, trial, and custody. At the posttrial stage with which this part of the report was concerned, the costs could only be averted if in fact the recidivist rate was reduced. Therefore,

. . . keeping the foregoing in mind, it is important to note that there appears to be no evidence of significant savings that will occur due to Community Corrections Centers operation.

If other detention institutions could be closed down, then the CCC would show savings on the criminal justice system. However, there will be extra costs rather than savings on the new CCC.

The imperfections of cost effective studies at this stage of our knowledge and expertise are highlighted by these examples. Often the kind of data necessary are not available in the form or pattern that would make assessment easier. Often the interrelationships are not clearly exposed for detailed examination, and the interflow between monetary costs and benefits and the other values involved is not fully traced. Nevertheless, the studies are provided here to indicate that the subject is being explored and that more can be expected to develop from the awareness of the fact that such approaches have significance and utility for the criminal justice system.

Planning, Programming, Budgeting System (P.P.B.S.)

This is an American invention that acquired currency as a result of its wide application in the U.S. Defense Department during the Vietnamese War. The P.P.B.S. is a kind of planning approach connected with budgeting in a country that does not have a national plan. This does not mean that it cannot be used in a country that has a national plan. But it has developed in America as a planning approach in situations where more comprehensive planning is not usual. It developed as a more rational method for the allocation of resources where each main department, responsibility, or area of concern of a given agency has had to find a better and more logical way of organizing its annual allocations of funds than the normal budget can be expected to provide.[e]

In national planning, the plan is usually prepared first and the annual budgets are then designed to fit into its framework. This is the pattern of planning with which the developing countries are most familiar and the system with which this paper has been mainly concerned. By contrast, in P.P.B.S. the planning takes off from the existing budget (i.e., instead of a development budget being designed according to a broad national objective). Assuming that no plan is available and the amounts for each year are already committed to a variety of established and existing projects, the P.P.B.S. works essentially with that 5-10 percent margin that is a normal increase in any budget in a developed country. The P.P.B.S. procedure requires that each agency or ministry makes an annual review of its own work in accordance with a special 5-year plan prepared for each of its main areas of responsibility. For each time phase, objectives are set and provided with (wherever possible) quantified indicators for each of which the necessary investments, equipment, personnel, etc. are set out. Priorities are also determined. Program budgeting forces the different levels of a bureaucracy to state objectives and the stages of approach to the achievement of these objectives, showing what will be needed at each level. Then the program is reviewed and brought up to date every year. Thus a Ministry of Health will prepare a 5-year plan for, say, malarial eradication or the provision of a minimum level of routine health care in rural areas.

Objectives will be set for each year in as quantifiable a form as possible and with specifications of the resources required at each stage; and orders or priority will be established, i.e., as to the geographical regions to be given first, second, or last attention or as to the intensity of spraying at different stages. The plan prepared by each ministry for each such area of responsibility will be so designed that the budgeting for the coming year will not only cover existing obligations but also provide for the first year of the new plan.

[e]Incidentally its use in federal government of the U.S.A. was brought to an end in 1971, but the idea continues to gather momentum elsewhere and was being adopted by the United Nations in the period 1973-1974.

However, in P.P.B.S. the plan—the preparation of which all administrators take a part in and set their own deadlines—is kept very tentative or provisional; and it can readily be changed as the situation changes, as new needs or unforeseen imperatives arise, and as the older approaches show themselves to be in need of revision. In this sense P.P.B.S. is a more pragmatic approach to planning than the broad national commitment to a total plan. In this sense it fits better the needs of a divided complex society that has not yet committed itself to national planning on the scale outlined in this paper. Moreover, in a government that has not been logically organized administratively and in which several departments, ministries, or agencies each carry only a part of the responsibility for a program (e.g., where the responsibility for child care or delinquency is distributed between Ministries of Health, Education, and Social Welfare), a planning approach to budgeting enables these different services to plan together to achieve their objectives via the usual budget.

Obviously, where a national plan for development exists, all this forward planning will have been done ahead, not only for each ministry but for the government and private sectors as well, and all the budgets will be geared to this national plan. The P.P.B.S. approach is not so directly applicable in this case; but nevertheless, its methods may help to clarify the implementation of the plan in annual stages.

P.P.B.S. makes very wide use of cost effectiveness concepts and other programming techniques and is perhaps far more applicable at the programming level, where goals are distinct and unequivocal. Its value lies in the way in which it organizes information flows and provides for systematic analysis, revealing the possible consequences of particular decisions before they are made. It requires, therefore, more use of social indicators and a more rational application of all the information available. It has been defined as a method of recosting the accounts of a government department in such a way that the budget is devoted to a number of determined programs.[f] Presumably, if P.P.B.S. becomes generally adopted by all agencies at all levels, it will eventually end up in a total national plan—but one produced from within the existing services rather than from any higher planning levels.

Other Techniques in Planning

The crime prevention planner, like his colleagues in other areas of national planning, will have recourse to any techniques that rationalize and systematize his task. Wherever possible he will seek to quantify or use models that are based upon given assumptions in certain situations. These are useful, providing he does not begin to mistake measurement for value or models for real situations. It is to be hoped that over the next few years the crime prevention planner will have a

---

[f]In this context a *program* is defined as an activity with a unique objective.

whole series of techniques based upon his own experience and designed to meet social planning and crime prevention planning needs—if not, indeed, to be extended to use in national planning as a whole.

Some National Experiences of Planning to Prevent Crime

It is difficult to provide actual examples of crime prevention planning in operation. For the reasons already given, it has barely surfaced in planning systems. In the terms of its definition here, there is no country engaged in comprehensive crime prevention planning. Most countries ignore it as a sector; and others, as we have seen, prefer to believe that this aspect of planning is covered by the more general provisions made for economic and social improvements. Even where more attention is given to the quality of life, this rarely includes special attention to crime.

At a more local or regional level, however, lessons are being learned from the concept of *defensible space* and from relationships between building patterns and crime. Often this too is immersed in wider programs for better community life and neighborhood development, which come back to the central problem of not giving crime sufficient attention in context.

The importance of law and order does not get lost, however, and examples are provided here in which the relationship between crime prevention and more general planning is thrown into relief. The countries given are types rather than cases on their own—except, perhaps, for the U.S.A. and China, which for many reasons may be regarded as cases in themselves. The U.S.A. is the one country that has felt that it had a sufficiently large problem of crime and sufficient funds to devote to a special agency; China appears to have adjusted its ideological inheritance to deeper indigenous social controls and traditions of longer standing in that society.

The intention here is to provide material for discussion rather than succinct examples of planning in action. The questions posed are centered on the results of present procedures and the need (if any) for broader approaches in future. What were the objectives (whether set in the form of planning discussed above or not); are they being achieved; are they being achieved by the methods adopted or incidentally? Are these unintended results? Some of these questions will be difficult to answer, but they lie at the center of any discussion of how to do better.

The United States of America

The United States Omnibus Crime Control and Safe Streets Act of 1968 [82 Stat. 197, 42 U.S.C.A. 3710 (1968)] was a deliberate attempt to prevent and control crime. There was no special national plan into which this legislation slotted, but Title I of the Act stated:

It is the purpose of this title to (1) encourage States . . . to prepare and adopt comprehensive plans . . . ; (2) authorize grants . . . to improve and strengthen law enforcement; and (3) encourage research and development of new methods for the prevention and reduction of crime and the detection and apprehension of criminals.

Now, seven years and billions of dollars later, with vast quantities of projects, research enterprises, and hardware gathering dust, the U.S. Attorney General has just announced a serious crime increase of 17 percent over last year. However, the record is uneven; there have been a large number of valuable investments made by the Law Enforcement Assistance Administration, which was set up by the Omnibus Act of 1968, and a great deal of experience has been gained that is now refining the present efforts to develop better planning for crime prevention. In particular, it has greatly improved the education of personnel dealing with crime; it aids over 1,000 facilities of law enforcement, criminology, or others dealing with crime; and it has developed a vast interest in the whole area of crime control; but the effects have not been what was hoped.

One distinction of great importance needs to be made. The United States has never regarded planning in this sense as running across all sectors in addition to its preoccupation with the crime inhibiting services like police, prisons, courts and corrections generally. Its idea of planning is, therefore, a good deal narrower than the sectoral planning for crime prevention outlined in this paper. Crime prevention planning in the United States is known as *criminal justice planning*, which amounts to an attempt to get planning within the police, corrections, and the courts, and to get the States to coordinate such plans. This, in itself, is quite an enormous task for 50 states of the size and importance of those in the U.S. It is a complicated procedure involving perhaps more vested interests and political influences than have been mentioned here.

At the same time and although the idea of criminal justice planning has been less extensive than that considered here as crime prevention planning, it is apposite that it need not be if a broader approach is required. Title I very generously defines law enforcement to mean "all activities pertaining to crime prevention or reduction, and enforcement of the criminal law."

Remembering then the difference in extension between the U.S. concept of *criminal justice planning* and the one developed here, it may be noted that four basic types of grants were provided for the states, to be funded out of Parts B, C, and E, of Title I of the Act:

1. Planning grants to assist the state to prepare annual, comprehensive criminal justice plans (Part B funds).
2. Action grants to support a wide variety of public protection projects (Part C funds).

3. Correction grants (Part E funds).
4. Discretionary grants to support experimental and special emphasis projects (i.e., 15 percent of total budget and administered directly by LEAA).

Other funds were provided by Title I (Part D) for training and education and in section 401 *et seq* for the creation of a National Institute of Law Enforcement and Criminal Justice. It is interesting to note that the Institute is authorized to make grants and contracts for the conducting of research and special projects pertaining to the purpose of Title I, to make continuing studies of approaches, systems, devices, techniques, and equipment designed to strengthen and improve law enforcement, to carry out programs of behavioral research regarding the causes of crime, the effectiveness of the various means of preventing crime, the effectiveness of correctional procedures, to make recommendations for action to improve and strengthen law enforcement, to create and grant research fellowships and special workshops, and to collect and disseminate information relating to new or improved approaches, etc.

The law was wide enough, but the experience was lacking. America had little experience in comprehensive national planning and none in crime prevention planning. The steady reduction of the approach to criminal justice planning often meant that emphasis was on the improvement of the police, courts, and corrections—and since there were too few studies of what might constitute improvement, the plans tended to be shopping lists of what departments wanted, e.g., to extend personnel, get better equipment, better education conditions, etc. A scrutiny of the first plans produced by the city of New York shows that while the police, courts, and corrections were represented on the committees approving plans, the plans were not coordinated, had no clear indication of purpose, and merely showed the projects each department felt it needed. These demands were then tailored to the availability of funds offered by the LEAA. In New Jersey, the LEAA funded the Criminal Justice Planning Agency and like those of other States, it became, in the words of a former assistant director, "a check writer for enforcement people." Thus "comprehensive" planning, according to the "Guide to Planning for Action" (Vol. I 1969) of the New Jersey agency, begins with the observation that criminal justice planning is conducted by one interrelated set of agencies—police, courts, prosecution, defense, and corrections. It does not take any wider perspectives.

Gradually, the defects of the drive to improve existing services and the ineffectiveness of simply meeting demands for "more of the same" as well as the evidence of additional personnel increasing bureaucracies without necessarily having an impact on the problem in the streets, elicited a greater sensitivity on the part of the granting agency to the need for better approaches to planning. A prestigious and well-funded National Advisory Commission of Criminal Justice Standards and Goals was set up to determine national objectives that local authorities could then relate in their own planning. This led to *crime oriented planning* as opposed to what had previously been termed *system oriented planning*. Improvements to the system had not been encouraging in the results on crime—now there was to be a more connected effort to reduce the levels of crime. The goals were seen as necessary, not merely to evaluate progress but to evaluate the planning for progress. For instance, one program director of a single project in New York—a community based drug center—when asked to state his aim in an application for funds, had no hesitation in giving a figure for the hard drug users that the center could service that was almost equivalent to the total population of the district within which the center was situated. In this case, evaluation showed the failure to choose realistic goals to begin with, so that the program was in constant difficulties.

The United States, with 50 states, some 4,000 or more police chiefs, and 55 or so major urban complexes, has an immense task to simply improve criminal justice planning and get viable criminal justice systems from so much uncoordinated work. Nevertheless, though not integrated into national planning of a more general type, it should be recognized that with its opportunity program to provide more job outlets and more satisfying types of work, with its extended welfare programs and housing and urban development schemes, and its Head Start and retraining programs for the unemployed, the United States has approached national planning in trying to do something about the social and economic environment for crime. Unfortunately, these efforts remain uncoordinated, and therefore conspicuously lacking in cross fertilization.

Some of the questions arising from the U.S. experience could be:

1. Would it really be too difficult to formalize some of LEAA's informal links with other departments of state with a view to producing a more comprehensive approach to crime prevention?
2. To what extent should the LEAA itself provide external planning for states that might be in difficulty whether in extending beyond the police courts and corrections or breaking out of local political complications?
3. How far can the experience of the LEAA in funding goal setting projects, housing renewals, educational programs, and the like be used to develop wider approaches to the crime prevention problem?
4. To what extent can the data from earlier investment in equipment and hardware be used to justify or discount the investments on software, i.e., rehabilitation programs, community involvement programs, etc. and vice versa?

China

In 1949 Mao Tse Tung called upon his Party to strengthen the police and the courts, as well as the army, because these were the State's major institutions for enforcing the people's democratic dictatorship.[6] The control of crime in China has depended upon far more than the increases in the criminal justice system, however. Thus 8 years later Mao Tse Tung argued that "disputes among the people" ought to be dealt with by:

... democratic methods, methods of discussion, of criticism, of persuasion, and education, not by coercive, oppressive methods.[7]

These two statements are perfectly reconcilable, of course, since the first was made at an early stage of the communist take-over and was directed at dealing with the "enemies of the state." While the later statement came when communism was more firmly established and internal problems, i.e., between people supporting the regime, were the point at issue.

In terms of historical progression, the control of crime seems to have been a combination of these two approaches—the development of informal controls for those who were not "enemies" and the use of more direct force for those who were "enemies." It should be observed, however, that with the lack of reliable information on China it is quite possible to be unfair or simplistic in the attempt to interpret what is known.

It is impossible, in communist terms, to differentiate between the measures taken to build the total society and those to deal with crime, but it would be a mistake to suggest the integration of crime control and development as proposed by this book is fully practiced. In communist countries, as in planning in the West, the broader plans have been expected to prevail over social problems like crime. Experience has shown the limitations of planning without direct and special attention to how crime prevention fits into the total planning process.

In the early stages of the revolution in China, there was the same confidence in total planning that had inspired all those taking Russia as a model. In 1953, when the drive in China was described as "transition to Socialism" and the First Five Year Plan began (though it was not fully worked out until 1955), there was belief in a better ordered, better organized, and progressively improving society by means of comprehensive planning:

With a naive confidence in rationality, which long ago disappeared in the West, they responded to the new slogans "regularize" (*zheng gui hua*), "systematize" (*zhi du hua*), and "rationalize" (*he li hua*) as if they were important steps on the road to utopia.[8]

By the end of 1957, 99.4 percent of the value of industrial output and 95.7 percent of the trade turnover was under state, joint, public-private, or cooperative ownership.[9] But the bureaucracy everywhere associated with centralized planning began to assert itself, introducing mistakes and an insensitiveness to local needs, which quickly generated local criticism and even resistence in some quarters. China with its traditionally autonomous regions was always a difficult country to control centrally and deeper rooted complications developed that cannot be fully discussed here. However, from the problems of the Great Leap Forward and the break with Russian patterns of central planning and bureaucracy, a more locally responsible type of planning has emerged over the years in China, the revision in terms of local needs being strengthened by the Cultural Revolution of 1966-1968.

That the comprehensive planning (even if localized) and major priorities of the government (industry over commerce, basic industry over consumer industry, long-term development over short-term comforts[10]) did not suffice of its own accord to deal with crime is shown by the separate attention paid to dealing with "enemies," "spies," and "saboteurs" in the early period and with "capitalist renegades" and "revisionists" later. Of course many of these were political opponents or party opposition that had grown up within the bureaucracy. But when every allowance is made for the blurring of terms like deviate or criminal, it has to be acknowledged that there were offenders against the penal code committing offenses that would have been dealt with in any country.

In the early period from 1949 and before planning proper had got under way, the main objective was to eliminate both political opposition and ordinary crime. The police stations were taken over by the army and reoriented as Public Security Bureaux with People's Disciplinary Teams of specially recruited full-time workers and volunteers working under the guidance of a company of the army in each district. These special teams patrolled their neighborhoods; similar groups of students were organized to patrol the schools and universities; and workers were mobilized to form full-time and voluntary teams to patrol places of work. Thus, according to the New China News Agency (Canton, Dec. 14, 1950), Canton had 7,214 security mutual aid teams under the direction of the police.[11] Of course, the precommunist police force had been weeded of its unreliable elements, and the rest had been sent to be politically educated. Often the police had power to take such action as they thought fit, and they first registered and later seized all firearms and occasionally had drives to arrest petty thieves, gamblers, opium addicts, whores, pimps, vagrants, and the like to hold them in long confinement, during which time they were reeducated or subjected to reform through labor. If released, they were supervised by the local security mutual aid team. Where side streets had doors that could be closed at night, this was done and in the very early period a curfew was imposed.[12]

Also the police rewarded those who informed on an offender and promised leniency for those who gave themselves up. Many, and especially those labelled counterrevolutionaries, were tried by kangaroo "peoples courts" at the local level or arraigned before the people in mass trials. Two ways, of course, in which the general political, economic, and social policies aided crime prevention policies were, first, that the process of reeducation inculcated a common pattern of values for all to follow and rewarded conformity as much as it punished deviance, and secondly, that since the authorities have control of basic food supplies, employment, and neighborhoods, it was extremely difficult for an offender to hide or subsist without regular work commitments.

In this period, therefore, while there was no conscious and clearly devised system for integrating planning for crime prevention (the first plan had not been launched), total control meant total crime prevention, with conventional criminals very likely to be treated more severely as political "enemies" if they did not take advantage of reeducation or yield to the tight neighborhood supervision.

Along with the adoption of the Russian planning model, the Chinese authorities moved between 1953 and 1957 to introduce a legal system that was similar to the Soviet Union's European-based system of inquisitorial judges, supervising the police and investigating as well as trying the cases. Here, rights were protected, police arbitrariness was controlled, and the courts set up were the exclusive determiners of criminal responsibility. This was a move towards an independent judicial system.[13] As China broke with Russia, the Party control of the legal system reasserted itself in a way that had never been possible in the Soviet Union, once the court bureaucracy had been established. Judges now consulted with Party Secretaries about their decisions, the public prosecutors gained court status at the expense of the accused, and the prosecutors were warned to abandon the "favor the accused" mentality that emphasized "troublesome legal procedures and the rights and status of the criminal, opening the door of convenience to the criminal."[14]

Since then, the trend has been to keep the legal system fluid and imprecise; to avoid exact definitions of crime or counterrevolution; to depend upon the pronouncements of Mao, party decisions, resolutions, orders, and policies; and China must be the only country in the world to have gone for so long without any exact legal definitions of offenses like murder, arson, robbery, rape, fraud, and theft. Yet, liability for these and other vague offenses can attract imprisonment, "reform through labor," seizure of property, loss of political rights, and even a death penalty (sometimes suspended). Consequently, the Soviets have criticized the Chinese looseness in definition of rights and protections as a mockery of socialist legality. Yet visitors to modern China are most impressed by the apparent absence of crime, by the honesty and law abiding nature of the people, and the complete security in which they live. Crime prevention may not have formed a conscious and distinct part of national planning—even criminal justice seems to be distinguished by its refusal to define limits and extensions—yet, the aim of most crime ridden cities elsewhere seems to have been achieved: China has no serious crime problems. This is not to say that China has no crime problems. The reports indicate not only problems with those who have learned to cheat the system but also with young people returning to the towns illegally from the rural areas and in difficulties without their grain rations. But when all the allowances for continuing crime problems have been made, it would be impossible not to acknowledge that China has, on any evidence or criteria, a good deal less crime than before the revolution and much less crime than many other countries.

The questions relevant to our interest are (a) how, and at what cost, was the Chinese control of crime achieved? (b) was it by planning or in spite of planning?

We know, immediately, that it is a control based on far more restriction or surveillance of movement than is typical of the West. From the early days there was a comprehensive registration of persons, households, births, marriages, deaths, divorce, employment, property, party relationships, etc.—and a very close supervision of everyone by the local street, courtyard, or neighborhood committees. We know that from the beginning it did not pay to be nonconformist. There were dangers of being labelled revisionist or renegade, and since political enemies were likely to be more severely dealt with than normal criminals, it was wise to avoid a political interpretation of ordinary crime. With the precision of a legal system virtually abandoned in the later stages, most trials not being public, and individual rights being devalued in relation to the prosecution, it must have been perilous in the extreme to have allowed oneself even to be suspected of deviation. Whereas in the West, in times of internal conflict, the label political crime is a claim for special treatment, i.e., not as ordinary criminals, in China there must have been a real danger of the ordinary offender getting far less consideration and more severe treatment if he courted the political label. As in other communist countries, the authorities sought to control behavior, attitudes, associations, and leisure down to the grass roots levels using neighbors' committees, street committees, students, workers, and activists in cadres to keep information flowing to the police. This kind of comprehensive control permeating all levels of society is the real cost of the Chinese success in dealing with crime.

This, with the refusal to be too specific about the definition of crime or the basic rights of anyone caught up in the network of control, represents a cost in crime control that some other countries have never been prepared to pay.

Quite early in the life of the regime the security forces fought a campaign against traditional secret societies in China (many of them on the periphery if not involved in criminal activities or the organization of criminal activities). By progressively eliminating the leaders using a variety of alienating techniques among the rank and file, the government succeeded in eliminating these divisive and sometimes criminal as well as subversive elements. Then, in controlling the lives of people, the government replaced these and many of the older social controls. With so much at stake, so little opportunity of attracting or mobilizing local (even neighborhood) sympathy, and virtually no protective legislation to either limit the powers of the authorities or provide a basis of individual rights, the offender or alleged offender was indeed exposed so that nonconformity meant everything that was menacing. Then, psychologically, it may be presumed that habit or conformity developed its own strength with rationalizations reinforcing the trend without any help from the authorities or the development of newer social controls. This, then, is the achievement—and its social and individual cost. To what extent was it done with or without planning?

As elsewhere, there was no integration of economic and social planning with crime prevention planning. But the interpretation of all these in political terms provided links, whether these links were intended or not. Though not consciously abstracted for separate planning attention, crime prevention is included when all behavior, even all thinking, is regarded as politically motivated and therefore subject to governmental direction and control. The fact that the authorities could control all employment, trade outlets, incomes, shopping, and the distribution of goods and food supplies generally—and did so with a particular interest in making sure that these could not be used to supply subversive groups likely to challenge the regime—means a form of crime control built into the system. The penetration of this control and alertness down to neighborhood, school, workshop, street, or courtyard levels with committees watching if not actually supervising residences and activities generally, meant that deviates and offenders of all kinds—including those who might associate with them, help, or sympathize with them—were all constrained at all times. The criminogenic potential was reduced by the reduction of the potential to act in any way unapproved or not tolerated by the government. In this sense it may be argued that there was planning.

On the other hand, China eventually repudiated both the centralized planning of the Soviets and its independent legal machinery protecting and guaranteeing the implementation of the constitution. Throughout its existence the Peking government has had difficulties dealing with its regionalized and traditionally autonomous country, so that localization has asserted itself. Moreover, this has been a tendency reinforced by the rejection of Soviet patterns and difficulties with budgets at the center.

China, therefore, is probably a unique example of loose, flexible, decentralized planning. The lack of definition of both a plan and a legal system work towards strengthening local power and authority; they facilitate arbitrariness but, by the same token, intensify local controls. For the real integration of crime prevention with more general economic and social planning in China, therefore, we need to look to the local levels. Here there is a supremacy of the Party organization, now that (since the Cultural Revolution) it has established itself over the bureaucracy. This, in itself, means a local integration of effort, whether to promote political, economic, and social development or to prevent crime. The relatively unrestrained power of the security forces and the lack of legal definition of limits allows them to exercise a control of behavior far wider than that which might be necessary for even a comprehensive control of conventional crime. The control of the means of production and distribution (in the absence of a rigid national plan) and the clarity of priorities of policy means an additional crime control measure. Thus, at the local level in China it is possible to conceive the whole organization of government—political, economic, and social—as being designed to prevent crime, not only conventional crime but any serious deviation from the approved norms. Or conversely, it is possible to consider the process of crime prevention (or norm fulfillment) as another way of achieving the political, economic, and social objectives.

There must of necessity be a great deal that is speculative about an analysis of this kind because of the dearth of reliable information. Perhaps a true appraisal will need to be written by a Chinese who knows the situation first hand—and who has access to official data. Meanwhile, the Chinese experience poses a number of vital questions for crime prevention planning anywhere else in the world.

1. Must effective crime prevention always be a part of the total political system? The Chinese do not really separate deviation from challenges to party authority. Does this mean that the effectiveness of crime prevention rises and falls with the political system? And, if this is true, is it possible to conceive of a kind of neutral crime prevention that works regardless of the political complexion of the government?

2. To what extent is the effectiveness of the Chinese crime prevention machinery due to the localized neighborhood control—which in any case had traditional roots in China?

3. Since the Chinese make such rigorous use of local committees at the street level to supervise behavior and student workers to oversee the conduct of colleagues, is this a *sine qua non* of good crime prevention? It must be observed that this is a system that has been used with equally impressive crime prevention results in most totalitarian states, and it operates informally in Japan, the only country with a falling crime rate concurrent with industrialization and urbanization.[15]

4. While great objection would be raised by all civil libertarians to the lack of a definition of criminal behavior, the unspecified limits to security authority, and the guaranteed protection of human rights by an independent judiciary, it may be that these have far less to do with the low crime rate of China than the encouragement of conformity and its inculcation by neighbors, friends, colleagues, and officials at all levels. It is doubtful whether the good behavior, honesty, and integrity of most Chinese can be written off as a mere function of repressive law enforcement, discrimination, and injustice. Has the regime found a way of mobilizing the natural tendency of a society to conform? If so, does the West pay too much attention to the ritualized safeguards; or does it actually encourage and reward deviation by its educational system (education for change), thereby building in some elements of conventional crime into its system?

5. Is the training of young people into conformity a *sine qua non* of a crime free society? This applies in simple tribal conditions where there is little or no crime; and it applies in societies with a value consensus like Moslem societies, where the crime rate is rarely high.

These are disturbing questions; but necessary ones for anyone concerned with crime prevention planning. Of course, an objective of a free society must be the maximum toleration consistent with the public good; but no one has drawn this line clearly. And whether the appeal is to law and order or to greater permissiveness, the line is bent to suit the argument. By looking at different societies we can look beyond the arguments about the line to the validity of the line itself. Perhaps it made good sense to be liberal about rights and individualism in law where there were strong social customs to ensure a measure of conformity. Maybe beyond a certain size and concentration of population this becomes unworkable. The fact that the greatest success in crime prevention has been by a virtual return to the collective responsibility of small local groups—even in large cities—suggests that it is less the law (repressive or permissive) that counts but rather social pressures that enable a society to maintain a direction without vacillating. The choice may not be between order and chaos, or tight or loose security, or even large or small forces for law enforcement; but rather the choice might well be between consistent and inconsistent values and clarity or confusion in their teaching and dissemination. Democracy has never really solved the problem of how far it can accommodate, unrestrained activities for the destruction of democracy. China gets itself into no such dilemma, but it pays a price that is heavy on the first generation but revalued by succeeding generations. Perhaps an appraisal will always have an ideological bias. Order and justice and freedom and safety do not coincide, and any planner has to select his own balance of interests.

Malaysia

Malaysia covers about 128,308 square miles and has two district regions separated by 400 miles of sea—the Malay Peninsula and the North Western coastal area of Borneo Island—Sabah and Sarawak. The total population of 10.5 million consists of Malays (50 percent), Chinese (37 percent), and Indians (11 percent), each group having its own linguistic, cultural, and religious background. As a politically independent nation, Malaysia dates from 1963 when it was a federation including Singapore. In August 1965 Singapore seceded, leaving Malaysia today a federation of 13 states. Since independence, this multiracial society has committed itself to the building of a united Malaysian nation with strength in its diversity. Its Second Malaysian Plan seeks to ensure that within two decades at least 30 percent of the total commercial and industrial activities (mainly exports of tin, rubber, timber, and palm oil with some light and medium industry) will be Malay in terms of ownership and management. According to its New Economic Policy the government seeks to ensure that no one will experience any loss, or feel deprived of his rights, privileges, income, or job opportunity. To this end a Nation Action Council has been established to implement the New Economic Policy. This consists of all

Cabinet members, the Chief Secretary to the government, the Chief of the Armed Forces Staff, and the Inspector General of Police.

Obviously, in the pursuit of the New Economic Policy the government is anxious to avoid the serious radical riots that took place in 1946 and 1969, and law and order, therefore, though not an express part of the total plan, gets special but separate attention. This explains the presence of the Army Chief and the Inspector General of Police on the National Action Council, which is charged not only with the implementation of the New Economic Policy but with the maintenance of national security by carrying out operations against terrorists. However, the National Action Council divides itself into the National Security Council and the National Economic Council, and the planning process does not unite them. Serving the National Action Council is a National Development Planning Committee under the Chairmanship of the Permanent Secretary to the Treasury; and to promote unity and a change in the older ways of thinking, great efforts are made in community development, popular education, and the eradication of illiteracy by the use of the media in all its forms. Alongside this, Goodwill Committees have been formed at all levels to help promote welfare locally and to keep order—or to cooperate with the police in doing so. In 1970, 80 percent of the 73 police posts ranging in cost from US$300 to US$800 were constructed by public donation. Police cadet corps are formed in secondary schools. As a special aid in addition to the usual judicial machinery, Malaysia has developed a quasijudicial procedure to deal with cases of secret societies, gangsters, and other dissidents against whom it might be difficult to collect evidence because of reprisals against witnesses. Such cases are investigated by the police and can then be referred to a judicial officer for inquiry. The judicial officer does not need to sit in a court for such a purpose and may, for example, use a hotel room. If the police substantiate a *prima facie* case, it is for the accused to explain himself to the satisfaction of the judicial officer. If a satisfactory and reasonable explanation cannot be given, the judicial officer recommends to the Minister of Home Affairs the issue of an order with special conditions. The person charged may, by this order, be either restricted to a particular area of the country or actually detained. If restricted, he may express a preference for the place he would like to be obliged to live under police supervision. If detained, it will be for a special term. The breach of any of the terms of an order makes the offender liable to imprisonment. There is a board of review that reconsiders the orders periodically. As a result of this quasijudicial procedure, it has been estimated that in Kuala Lumpur alone the crime rate fell by 50 percent in 1969.

Similarly, Malaysia uses the discretionary powers of the Criminal Procedure Code to deal with habitual offenders by subjecting them to police supervision for 3 years after sentence. Actually, Malaysia, due to its peculiar history, has one of the most complex systems of statute law in the world. It has laws passed by forty different legislatures including:

1. Prewar Ordinances of the Straits Settlements (still in force in Penang and Malacca).
2. Prewar Enactments of the Federated Malay States.
3. Ordinances of the Malayan Union.
4. Ordinances of the Federation of Malay.
5. Enactments of the Nine Malay States and the two Settlements from 1948 to Merdeka Day 1957.
6. Ordinances of North Borneo and Sarawak before Malaysia Day.

A revision of the Laws Act 1968 provides for a continuous law revision machinery by a special Commission. An Anticorruption Agency has been active in dealing with some 17,000 complaints between 1967 and 1970 alone, and several hundreds of persons have been prosecuted, including government servants, police, and legal officers. All government officers are required to declare all assets on entry to the service and to report every later acquisition.

Originally, the Anticorruption Agency in Malaysia was a small specialized branch or unit of the police. In 1963 it was placed under a legal officer with a Royal Charter and made responsible only to the Minister of Home Affairs. After 3 years of publicity campaigns and operations by undercover agents the Agency has eventually got government servants cooperating with them in reducing corruption. The agency receives about 400 allegations daily, of which, it has been suggested, only 2 percent are without substance. It has also been said that the corruption involves only 1 percent of the government servants who in turn are 2 percent of Malaysia's total population.[16]

Some questions arising from the Malaysian experience might be:

1. To what extent is the day-to-day work of the two subcommittees of the National Action Council allowed to overlap? Is there coordination at least in the determination of capital investments on the criminal justice services?
2. How far is the unification drive working? In other multiracial societies conflicts have been avoidable only by insulating the country from outside influences and limiting communications.
3. To what degree is this a repressive system in Malaysia? Does the criminal justice system bear down on some groups unfairly?
4. How could the Malaysian New Economic Policy be reframed to incorporate crime prevention more directly?

The Malaysian experience cannot really be cited as an example of planning for crime prevention, in the sense of an intersectoral attempt to deal with the criminogenics of society; but, as a result of its troubles, Malaysia is an example of a purposeful attempt to link, if not integrate, the action being taken to build a united Malaysia with law and order measures. How far it will work, the extent to which special measures are justifiable, and the problems peculiar to Malaysia cannot be discussed here. Suffice to add, however, that Malaysia is one of the countries that has recently been claiming a wider measure of success in crime control.

Poland

Poland is a country that has already been mentioned as having the U.S.S.R. type of machinery for the comprehensive planning of the economy. In this sense it plans *inter alia* to prevent crime. However, the crime prevention work is not a separate part of the national planning; it is assumed to be inherent in all the other plans that are prepared for much wider purposes. To get some idea of crime prevention policies in Poland, therefore, it is necessary to look at its criminal justice system. Information is not as readily available as one might wish, but there has been a recent attempt to revise and review the criminal policy, which is of interest in showing both attitudes and expectations.

In Poland, as in other countries with a socialist (Communist) system, the basic tenet that informs all planning is that improvements in economic and social conditions will remove the reasons for crime and therefore greatly reduce the problem, if not indeed eliminate it altogether. On the one hand, there is no specialist crime prevention planning; on the other hand, it is claimable that all the national and comprehensive planning for better social and economic conditions is crime preventative. It has been shown that this is not necessarily automatic, either in the West or in the developing areas of the world, but Poland has statistics to indicate that after the introduction of the new social order in 1945 crime has shown a steady decline. It is pointed out that in Poland between 1932 and 1937 the average number of convictions was 175 per 100,000 people, whereas in the period 1964 to 1968 the average was 109 per 10,000.[17]

However, Poland still has crime problems, particularly with hooligans, juvenile delinquents, and offenses related to alchol. In 1969, therefore, a new Penal Code was enacted, which introduced a new kind of criminal policy. Harsher punishments were provided for serious offenders than those obtaining before 1970, but also more measures were adopted for minor infringements of the law. A number of minor offenses were decriminalized by this code, such as failing to send a child to school; others, like traffic offenses (including driving under the influence of drink), were regarded as violations of administrative regulations and not crimes. Also the new Code allowed the conditional discontinuance of proceedings by the prosecutor or the court at a preliminary hearing where the offense is not punishable by more than 3 years imprisonment and the character and environment of the offender indicate that he is unlikely to offend again—and where he is prepared to apologize to the victim, compensate him, and perform work of a community nature for a specified test period. Another requirement, however, is that the state organization to which the offender belongs—or some other agency or person—pledge to exercise influence over the offender to avoid future trouble.

Included in this less severe approach to the less serious offenses is a new kind of probation or suspended sentence (often subject to a pledge as above), during which period a person cannot, without the court's permission, change his address, take part in social functions or organizations, and may be required to do unpaid public work for a term of not less than twenty and not more than fifty hours per month. This obligation to perform unpaid public work may be substituted by corresponding reductions in salary (10 to 25 percent) if the offender is employed already in a state enterprise. This idea—community work or deduction of earnings—is regarded as an extension of the notion of a fine. The Code raises fines considerably and extends the sanction of a confiscation of property. Again, without the court's permission the offenders under restricted and supervised liberty must not discontinue their work, cannot get a salary increase or promotion, and may be required to apologize to and compensate the victim.

At the other end of the scale, the new Code raised minimum statutory penalties for a number of offenses (e.g., in the Code of 1932 the minimum statutory penalty for murder was 5 years and this is raised to 8) and allowed an increase of the sentence for recidivists (in some cases not less than 2 years additional regardless of the type of offense). Protective supervision and enforced stays at social readaption centers are also measures adopted for recidivists in addition to the penalty for the offense, though whether these are to be regarded as penalties under the law or protective measures are still being debated in legal circles in Poland. For hooligans, who are specially defined by Article 120 para 14, the minimum penalties are raised by 50 percent, and in addition to compensation the offender may have to pay to the victim a special amount of financial redress—not commensurate with the damage done.

To reduce short-term imprisonment the minimum statutory imprisonment was raised from 1 week to 3 months, and a fine was substituted for imprisonment in a large number of minor offenses. And to make the offender responsible for the costs of his own imprisonment, the new Penal Code arranges some institutions in such a way that the offender is obliged to cover the costs of his incarceration. All inmates are required to work, and a considerable part of their earnings is deducted for their maintenance plus 5 percent extra to cover after-care services.

Ninety percent of the criminal cases in Poland are tried by a single professional judge sitting with two lay judges who have equivalent powers so that there is a wide degree of public participation in the awarding of sentences. In the execution of sentences outside of institutions there is, as we have seen, a need for appropriate responsible persons or institutions to pledge themselves for the future good behavior of the offender. It may be imagined that in the conditions of a fully organized society such as is typical of the socialist, communist states these pledges are powerful restraints on the individual offender, who has to fit into the system to survive.

The New Penal Code of Poland came into operation on 1 January 1970. From 1965 to 1972 the average number of adults convicted by Polish courts was about 210,000 (for a population of some 32 million) and 500,000 persons a year were dealt with in quasicriminal proceedings by the various administrative authorities. Not surprisingly, as a result of the new Code, there was in 1970-1971 an increase in the cases dealt with administratively. In 1970 the conditional quashing of proceedings was applied by courts in 8,591 cases and in 1971 in 5,154 cases. By prosecutions it was applied to 26,000 cases in 1970, and to about 30,000 cases in 1971. On the other hand the new form of suspended sentence or restricted liberty, though applied in 10,325 cases in 1970 and 18,349 in 1971, seems to have been falling by 1972.

It is appreciated that this account of the modified criminal policies introduced by a new Penal Code is not strictly speaking an example of planning. It is provided here, however, because with comprehensive national planning as a background to the changes in criminal policy, they do bear a relationship. Poland offers a case similar to Malaysia, where the criminal justice system is used to uphold and promote national objectives so, for example, alterations in sentencing policy have planning implications.

The Polish information could be discussed around the following questions:

1. If the comprehensive planning is being effective, what were the reasons for the changed policy. The laws needed updating, but the principles adopted are obviously suggested by actual needs, e.g., have harsher punishments proved effective with the recidivist in the past? Is this why the incidence of crime fell? If not, why is the increased sentence necessary now?
2. The socialist system provides for integrated planning, but crime prevention is not usually a separate planning sector. Is then the revised policy a reflection of separate and independent thinking by the lawyers?
3. Should systems of correction be self-supporting?
4. Are centrally planned economies with uniform ideologies in a better position to develop powerful community alternatives?

Conclusions

As this book is wound up, a note of warning should be sounded about the danger of being carried away by planning. The need for a humility is ever present, and there always needs to be someone who evaluates and assesses not only the planners but the evaluators themselves. It is all too easy for a new mystique of the white-coated specialist in planning and evaluation to be fostered, and for him to be regarded as the modern medicine man with all the answers. This was the aura that once surrounded research but which is now a trifle jaded because the millions of dollars spent on crime research have not produced the magic prophilactic. The elitism can easily shift to the planner or evaluator if care is not taken to keep them all firmly grounded. In the general context of crime as a social phenomenon, which has been the approach of this book, it would not be difficult to see planners and evaluators as themselves deviate from the social norm, since they seek to set themselves up as special organizors or in judgment of others. Such reflections help to keep a healthy balance in the approach suggested here. The complexities and underlying assumptions are never to be overlooked or minimized. Still it is obvious that other approaches to crime control have been even more disastrous. A monolithic dedication to law and order or social discipline or a morally self-righteous attitude no less than the veiled patronizing of much penal reform has ignored whole dimensions of the crime problem. A dedication to deviance and the right to be different, if carried to extreme permissiveness, postulates a faith in the goodness of human nature, which experience does not substantiate.

Crime prevention planning is a new approach and a novel form of expertise, which will attract planners, architects, economists, sociologists, and criminologists in the years to come. This first approach is an attempt to survey the ground rather than to cultivate each part of it. It is intended to provide an orientation for the beginner in this field. Its writing had underlined the fact that it needs followup at every stage, because even to fulfill its modest purpose it could not be extensive enough, sufficiently intensive, or even adequately polemic. If it serves only to introduce a new and more balanced thinking about crime as something integral to a society, it will have served its purpose. When people are murdered, robbed, exploited, or exposed to boisterous hooliganism of one kind or another, they tend to think of crime as a disorder or abnormality to social life. That it may be; but it is also a built-in phenomenon that takes different shapes at different times or in different places. It does not have to be so dangerous or disturbing if it is dealt with at the time of its instigation or discouraged by the kind of society we are developing.

Of course, there will always be perverse or pathological characters, but they can be constrained by a society better developed and equipped to deal with them. Their numbers can be reduced by better planned education, health, and welfare services. There will always be deviates who contribute to, as well as despoil, the community. Once again the channels for their deviate potential need not be so wide or so restricted as to force them to act out their deviations on others or to the detriment of others. Even the aggressive potential of a society can be sublimated by better physical, economic, and social planning.

The older repressive remedies or unthinking permissive remedies for crime will be displaced by more balanced, humanitarian, but less idealistic or sentimental, approaches to the problem. Criminals should not be our scapegoats carrying the sins of those who are either too inhibited to attempt what the offenders have dared—or who perhaps have succeeded in avoiding exposure and prosecution. They are not completely evil, nor again are they the only evil persons in our midst. On the other hand, they are not saints, or the products of underprivilege, to be treated with such indulgence and sympathy that their victims are stigmatized for daring to report them. All these are aberrations in the prevention and treatment of crime, which derive from the inability to see crime as largely our own creation, whether by faulty child care, injustice, ineffective schooling and guidance, poor health care, the failure to provide fulfilling work opportunities, or the break-down of a basic system of values. And they often oversimplify (by over-harsh or over-indulgent short-term expedients) the longer-term task of planning for a more rational and wholesome future for people, generally, and offenders, in particular. In the same way, the suggestion that crime is a simple function of power distribution and therefore attributable to a vicious capitalism or a repressive communism overlooks the relativity of crime, the obdurate prevalence of human nature, and the fact that no society has eliminated crime altogether. We have to plan for less crime—not for no crime—for a better society and not for utopias, which fascinate but always flit beyond our reach.

In the past, crime has been the work of the devil to be ousted by grace; the creation of our economic system to be cured by revolution; the fault of our childhood repression to be solved by indulgence; or the result of deprivation to be cured by affluence. Now it is the fault of our criminal justice system to be resolved by decriminalization and a higher regard for human rights—to be deviant if so disposed. Whatever the point of view, whatever the angle on crime one may wish to take, it remains true that crime will be better prevented than cured. Individual prevention will depend upon the particular situation and the proportions of nature and environment, socialization, or will. But, in general, and whatever one's point of view, crime prevention means bringing crime and its prevention more effectively into the focus of national planning.

Notes

1. From *Thailands Budget in Brief: Fiscal Year 1971*. It should be noted that the total budget appropriation for the year was 28,645 baht.

2. W.M. Landers, "An Economic Analysis of the Courts," *Journal of Law and Economics*, April 1971, pp. 61-107.

3. J.J. Vanecko, "Community Mobilization and Institutional Change," *Social Science Quarterly*, 50, no. 3, 1969.

4. Michael E. Borus, *The Economic Effectiveness of Retraining the Unemployed* (New Haven: Yale University Press, 1964). See also "A Benefit-Cost Analysis of Retraining the Unemployed," *Yale Economic Essays*, Fall 1964, vol. 4, no. 2, pp. 371-429.

5. See *A Handbook on Community Corrections in Des Moines*, U.S. Department of Justice, Law Enforcement Assistance Administration, National Institute of Law Enforcement and Criminal Justice.

6. Address by Mao Tse Tung, "On the People's Democratic Dictatorship," 1940; reprinted in *4 Selected Works of Mao Tse Tung* (Peking: 1961), pp. 411-418. Quoted by Jerome Alan Cohen in "The Criminal Process in the People's Republic of China: An Introduction," *Harvard Law Review*, Jan. 1966, p. 471.

7. Address by Mao Tse Tung, "On the Correct Handling of Contradictions Among the People," 1957; reprinted in *Collection of Laws and Regulations of the People's Republic of China*, 1 (Peking, 1957), pp. 5-6. Quoted by Jerome Alan Cohen, *Chinese Meditation on the Eve of Modernization*, 54, 1966, p. 1200.

8. Ezra F. Vogel, op. cit., p. 126.

9. Ibid., p. 173. Quotation from Canton, Joint Publications Research Service, U.S. Department of Commerce, No. 16369:27.

10. Ibid., p. 71.

11. Ibid., p. 67. Quotation from Survey of China Mainland Press, U.S. Consulate, Hong Kong.

12. Ibid., p. 61.

13. Jerome Alan Cohen, "The Criminal Process in the People's Republic of China: An Introduction," *Harvard Law Review*, Jan. 1966, pp. 479-483.

14. Ibid., p. 484.

15. See W. Clifford, *Crime Control in Japan* (Lexington, Mass.: Lexington Books, D.C. Heath and Company, 1976).

16. Hassan Bin Ishah, *Criminal Justice System in Malaysia: The Anticorruption Agency*, UNAFEI Resource Materials, Series No. 2, Tokyo, Japan.

17. P. Mackowiak and S. Ziembinski, "Social Aspects of Sources of Criminality and its Prevention and Control," *International Review of Criminal Policy*, 29, 1971.

Postscript:
Planning Crime Prevention
in Australia

This book has many limitations, simply because it represents a groping after concepts and ideas that have become conspicuous because planners have given them insufficient attention. It aims at practice, however, and what was set forth in the foregoing chapter is being taken seriously in Australia. A full account of this work, which is now in progress, would require another book. But a brief survey here will indicate to those who might be concerned with the problem of applying the ideas, that crime prevention *is* being attempted.

Australia, one of the world's oldest land masses, is important for crime because of its origins as a convict colony. For centuries before 1770 when it was discovered by Captain Cook, it had been known to map makers as *Terra Australia Incognita.* It had not been found but it was known to be there. When it was discovered, it took nearly 20 years for a decision to be made on its settlement. Then on August 18, 1786 Lord Sydney wrote a letter to the Lords Commissioners of the Treasury in which he said:

The several goals and places for the confinement of felons in this kingdom being in so crowded a state that the greatest danger is to be apprehended, not only from their escape, but from infectious distempers, which may hourly be expected to break out among them, His Majesty, desirous of preventing by every possible means the ill consequences which might happen from either of these causes, has been pleased to signify to me his royal commands that measures should immediately be pursued for the sending out of this kingdom such of the convicts as are under sentence or order of transportation.

Of course with the American colonies lost, there was a need to find an alternative place of exile. Thus on 31 May 1787 the first group of ships left England with 759 convicts (20 percent women), 206 marines, with the rough total of 1,000 being made up by servants, various officials, and children. Most of the convicts were being transported for property offenses, and most of them were from London or nearby cities—then beginning to suffer from the growing pains of urbanization. There were said to be no political offenders among them. They starved, suffered great hardships, and many died before the new settlement became viable. But from what England had considered to be its human offal, the overspill of its bulks and prisons, there arose modern Australia, the size of the United States, with nearly 14 million inhabitants, 50 percent of whom live in Sydney and Melbourne and who are comprised of, besides the British, Italians, Greeks, Germans, Dutch, Poles, Maltese, Turks, Cypriots, Arabs, Chinese, Koreans, Filipinos, Thais, Vietnamese, and many others.

With its industries, mines, ports, and commerce, Australia is an economically developed country with natural resources as yet to be exploited fully. On the other hand, with its sheep farming, beef production, fruit, and wheat, it is also a country of primary products. It is not therefore a fully developed country in the sense of having the great urban over-sprawls that characterize some of the greater powers (though Sydney and Melbourne are beginning to approximate some of these). On the other hand, it is not a "developing" country in the sense that it lacks the resources for development. As an in-between nation, therefore, it is a very special type of country for the application of the kinds of planning techniques described in the foregoing pages. And it was partly for this reason that the author was recruited from the United Nations in 1974 to become Director of the new Institute of Criminology, created as a statutory authority by the states and the federal governments of Australia. It was to become a resource center for the authorities at state and federal levels, charged with the prevention of crime and the treatment of offenders. For, while crime levels had not reached those of some of the countries of the West, the cities were being plagued by growing crime rates, and all the problems of the urban West were afflicting the Australian cities.

In 1970 when an Australian delegation attended the Fourth United Nations Congress on the Prevention of Crime and the Treatment of Offenders held in Kyoto, Japan, it was greatly attracted by the idea of planning crime prevention, which had been a principal theme of the Congress. As a result of the reports of this delegation, at least one state (Western Australia) had established a committee for social defense planning, which, however, because it lacked planning expertise has gradually become defunct.

As soon as the new Institute found its feet, however, it began to move into the planning arena. Australia does not have national economic and social planning in the full sense of that term. This is not to say that it has no nationwide economic and social policies, because some of these in health, education, and welfare are quite impressive. But national sectoral planning as it has been conceived here is not in operation. There were in Australia, however, a number of schemes for growth areas to relieve the pressures on the rapidly growing cities—and some of these cities were themselves taking the limited opportunities offered for replanning the central areas. Here, then, in both physical and regional, or zonal, planning projects were the opportunities for testing some of the ideas that this writer has been propagating via the United Nations and international meetings. At the time of this writing the Australian Institute of Criminology is perhaps the first Institute of its kind anywhere in the world that is beginning to work in close harness with local planning authorities in the hope of reducing the crime problems for the next generation if not indeed for the next decade. In 1974 a start was made with a special seminar held jointly by the Institute and the Development Corporation for Albury-Wodonga, a growth center being planned on the borders of the states of New South Wales and Victoria. In 1976 a project was designed by the Institute in conjunction with the people and local authorities of Geelong, a growth center situated on the coast of Victoria, outside Melbourne. These are described below. Arrangements have already been made for a more ambitious project at Bathurst-Orange, a growth center in New South Wales. At very early stages of negotiation are a similar scheme for the incorporation of crime prevention planning into the redevelopment of a Sydney dock area known as Woolloomooloo and for a broader approach in 1977 to the planning of crime prevention in the area of Adelaide and its suburbs in South Australia. These are early days and the outcome cannot be forecast with any confidence, but a start is being made to find practical applications for the ideas in this book.

Albury-Wodonga

A seminar in one week's duration was planned by the Institute of Criminology with the Albury-Wodonga Development Corporation in April or May of 1974, with a view to convincing the authorities responsible for the planning in this area—and the local communities—to include planning for less crime in the general development of the area. Arrangements were being made for people from the twin towns of Albury-Wodonga to join with planners, criminal justice personnel, and representatives of health, education, and welfare from all the other states of Australia in a study of the local problem and the prospect for the future. A group of senior students from local high schools were included. Public meetings were held at the two city centers at the beginning and end of the seminar. The seminar itself consisted of a number of specialized workshops dealing with particular aspects of the future planning.

Albury and Wodonga are small separate towns, one in New South Wales and the other in Victoria, but they are divided by the River Murray, which forms the state boundaries. The idea for the future is to develop this area so that it will grow from its present population of 50,000 to 300,000 in 25 years. Arrangements are being made to attract industry, commerce, and government centers to the area, and there are plans for new housing, a university, colleges of advanced education, and new roads and forms of communication. A report on the proceedings of this seminar[1] is available, and although I do not propose to repeat it here, some of the recommendations for implementation were:

1. The various agencies for social control (police, prisons, and probation offices) should not be perceived as existing in isolation from the community but as integral parts of it. Special representative committees were proposed to participate in the planning.
2. The media should become not only a vehicle for community education in crime prevention but a means of building up a sense of community.
3. In planning physical facilities care should be taken to avoid the development of deprived neighborhoods with few available services. A mix of housing styles (public and private) and of age groups should be fostered. The grouping of single-parent families together was felt to be inappropriate in

terms of possible stigmatization. Dormitory suburbs connected with industrial development should be avoided.

4. Schools should become community facilities available for the after-school activities of children and the continuing education of adults.
5. Offenders should be treated as far as possible within the local community. There were recommendations for nonresidential assessment centers, a special remand center, and the reliance on probation and semicustodial treatment with the possibility of a small prison for no more than 80 persons being deferred until it was found to be unavoidable.
6. Public transport should not be operated on a purely economic basis but should be subsidized to augment community development.
7. Police forces in Albury-Wodonga should have reciprocal rights and powers in both areas to overcome interstate jurisdictional and border problems.
8. Opportunities for crime could be reduced by specified simple precautions at home, in shops, and in factories. There should be visible security checks at supermarkets and poor street lighting should be improved.
9. It was thought possible, without encroaching on the privacy of inhabitants to subdivide interior areas in the residential districts to increase a sense of neighborliness and to ensure that lobbies, paths, and hallways were well lit and overlooked by tenants from their windows.
10. Discrepancies in legislation and local administration as a result of having two cities, two states, the Australian Assistance Plan, the federal government, and the Albury-Wodonga Development Corporation involved in the planning were thought to be conducive to crime—not only conventional crime but also white-collar crime. It was thought that this ought to be resolved.

It should be remembered that these were local people sitting with specialists in government services who made these recommendations. They were not professional planners. The professional planning for crime prevention was to follow as a result of the Chairman of the Albury-Wodonga Development Corporation's closing address, in which he invited the Institute of Criminology to continue the work it had begun by the seminar. Replying for the Institute the Assistant Director hoped that it would be no more than the "end of a beginning."

Geelong

While Albury-Wodonga had been a useful exercise of a nationwide character to arouse interest in crime prevention planning and had established the basis for future collaboration with the planning authorities, the Institute felt that it should do more to focus techniques on a selected area and community. This opportunity appeared when the Institute was invited to organize a joint project with the people of Geelong in the state of Victoria. Here there was more time for preparation, and several months before the meetings at Geelong in February 1976 the Institute staff worked with local people preparing specific data to present to the several workshops.

The Geelong region in Victoria is one of the three major growth centers in Australia, the others being Albury-Wodonga, already discussed, and Bathurst-Orange in New South Wales. In all of these there is a rapid increase in population and social problems. Geelong, which is situated on the south coast of Australia about 30 minutes along a first-class coastal highway from the large city of Melbourne, is therefore a suburb of Melbourne. But it is far enough away to have developed its own characteristics and industries, and it is also a grain exporting center for the rural hinterland. The town of Geelong itself encompasses Cario Bay but the Geelong Planning Region extends well inland to include South Barwon, Bellarine, Barraboo, Cario, and Bannockburn.

The data prepared in advance of the meetings by the Institute and its Geelong collaborators from the local authorities, planning, social welfare, educational, and health services showed that the regional population had expanded in the post-Second World War period at a rate only exceeded in the period 1850-1870. The combined impact of immigration, natural increase, and migration within Victoria and the growth industry in Geelong had led to a sustained growth of population in the 1950s and early 1960s. There had been a drop in population growth in the late 1960s related to the fact that planned capacity in manufacturing and peak workforces had been reached and to the singularity that tertiary sector (which was the major growth sector in the national economy) had not grown quite so much in Geelong. At the time of the project the average population growth rate was 1.78 percent, but for some years Geelong had had twice the national average of unemployment.[a]

In the postwar period the number of people in the Geelong Planning Region, i.e., living in the urban-suburban area of Geelong, had grown from 63.3 percent of the total population of the region in 1947 to 73.5 percent in 1971. And in the last decade more people have moved into the coastal and peninsular towns. So that while the rural areas and smaller rural towns had had stable populations, younger people had been moving to the more urbanized areas. There had been an immigration from overseas comparable to that of Melbourne. Geelong has the highest proportion (22.2 percent) of foreign-born people of all the provincial regions of the state of Victoria. Most of these were people from English speaking countries (37.3 percent). Others were mainly Yugoslav, Italian, Dutch, German, and Austrian people. And most concentrated in the Geelong Urban Area—looking for industrial employment. The areas of residence for these persons was traced for the purpose of the study.

[a]This and the rest of the demographic outline that follows was provided by Peter Hocking of the Geelong Regional Planning Authority, whose paper "Population Parameters of the Social Fabric of the Geelong Region," which was specially prepared for the Institute's Geelong project, will be published in the Institute's forthcoming report of the project.

In absolute figures, between 1966 and 1971 about 25,000 people moved into the Geelong Region and 20,000 or so moved out—giving a net gain of 5,000. This seemed to show that young people, educated and trained within the region, were moving out to find employment elsewhere. These were the professionally or technically trained, the administrators, executives, and managerially trained as well as clerical workers—reflecting the slowness of the growth of the tertiary sector in Geelong and its more rapid growth elsewhere in the country. A large number of those moving into the region were found to be unskilled or semiskilled in the 25 to 34 year age group and usually with families of young children under 9 years of age. Another population move relevant to crime prevention was the number of nonmetropolitan migrants coming into the region for from 1 to 3 years.

The population structure of the Geelong Urban area reflected the physical development and structure it encouraged. Thus, the older, inner areas of Geelong City, Geelong West, and Newtown had fairly high proportions of people over 45 years of age, despite the fact that even in these areas the largest single age group was the 15 to 24 year age group. This was said to result from the movement into town areas of young single people and of young rural-urban migrants attracted by the availability of older rental houses and the large number of flats (apartments) built in the last 10 years. This older housing inner area had also attracted the non-English-speaking immigrants at the reception stage. Geelong West had been a center for Italian born immigrants, and from this area there had been little movement out in recent years. Newtown had been traditionally a high socioeconomic status area, despite the fact that it had a number of small single-fronted timber housing units. But since 1971 there have been some replacement of this housing with flats, and as a result a movement in by the young, single, and married people.

As opposed to this structure for the inner city areas, the newly developed outlying areas of Corio, South Barwon, and Bellarine were dominated by the younger age groups. These areas had absorbed the bulk of regional growth after the war and have large numbers of young families with the highest proportion of school aged children.

To get some idea of the development of crime in recent years in the region a study was made of total offenses cleared by the police in the region for 6 months of 1970 and 6 months of 1974. In all it seemed that crime reported to the police annually was averaging 5,000 or so cases. In 1970 there had been no homicides cleared, and in 1974 only one. However, total crime (on the basis of this admittedly inadequate data) had risen by 48.8 percent, i.e., during a period when the population increase was about 6.02 percent. Projecting this over the next decade, it was clear that if the trend continued it would not only present a problem of crime greater than had been anticipated, but a problem for which only inadequate provision in estimates was now being made. The areas where offenders lived roughly correlated with the newly developed outlying areas where young people of school ages predominated.[2] Not surprisingly, the city center emerged as the most highly victimized area, with a rate of offenses committed there four times higher than any other. Only 8.9 percent of the offenders were female. The highest category of offenders were the unskilled—but students were the next highest group. Seventy percent of all offenders were born in the state of Victoria, and a further 10 percent were born elsewhere in Australia. This left only 20 percent of offenders foreign born; the two major offending groups in this small number were British and Yugoslav. Two-thirds of all the offenders committed their offenses alone. In less than 9 percent were there two offenders working together, and in only 4.8 percent of the cases were there more than two offenders involved. This suggested that Geelong had, as yet, only a very limited problem of gang delinquency.

The above is only a selection of the material prepared for the seminar. This time the Institute concentrated its efforts on cooperation with local planners and officials. Again there were public meetings before and after the workshops, but only one or two specialized outsiders were invited to participate in the workshops—one of these having been concerned with the exercise at Albury-Wodonga the previous year. This preinvestigation and concentration of effort on the Geelong area meant that workshops were more tightly focused. As a result the recommendations were more direct than at Albury-Wodonga and of more direct use for planning purposes. The full report has not yet been published, but some of the recommendations were:

1. The planning process itself in the Geelong Planning Region needed revision to permit more coordination. A disparity was identified between the meaning of regionalization in Geelong and in the centers of state and federal government. Sometimes in the allocation of available resources for health, education, and welfare the local interests were not adequately consulted. Regionalization meant more than the decentralization of government offices—it meant a greater degree of local authority and autonomy.

2. The increase of 2 percent per annum in population contrasted with the constancy of an unemployment rate double the national average showed a structural problem of unemployment related to the undiversified nature of local industry—this needed attention.

3. The wheel-based economy of the area penalized the young people without transport. Most of those giving trouble came from outlying areas without any local entertainment or diversions and for whom the last bus left at 10 P.M. This could be improved by planning to supply the outlying areas with leisure facilities—and by either planning for a wider spread of transportation or planning to reduce the dependence on vehicles. A large proportion of offenses were related to car stealing, drunken driving, etc.

4. The media could be deeply involved in planning for crime prevention in the future without interfering with its freedom to make news available to the

public. Taking, for example, the involvement of a local paper in "Safety City," a campaign to reduce death on the roads, the group thought that the media could cooperate with crime prevention planning groups not only to report crime but to make the public aware of the deeper and longer-term damage of crime in terms of its social and economic costs.

5. The present ratio of 1:880 police per head of population could be allocated more effectively to achieve a better police-public relationship. This would mean decentralized precincts of the C.I.D., the restoration of suburban police stations, and more community involvement in nonspecific police work. It was recognized that good police work depended upon a smooth flow of information, so that the police could serve rather than control local community. The above measures were aimed at making the police-community relationship closer and the process of information giving less tedious and troublesome.

6. Legislation should be streamlined to remove from the police nonspecific duties. In a local context this meant the removal from the police of the Motor Registration Branch, License Testing, and Traffic Control, including speed traps and all "noncriminal" traffic offenses.

7. There should be a study undertaken over a period of 5 years to establish the social and economic costs of crime in Geelong.

8. The isolation of school and community—a process that often occurs both ways should be broken down. At present there is in Geelong a lack of community access to, or participation in, school facilities and activities and, it was observed, schools rarely follow up evidence of criminal tendencies or make adequate references to community agencies. This was followed by a number of specific changes needed locally to effect this integration of functions.

9. There should be a wider distribution of future employment opportunities in such a way as to reduce the overconcentration of particular income and occupational groups in certain areas. This should include the early expansion of the tertiary sector.

10. Since past investigations have shown a serious lack of knowledge by students about to leave Secondary Schools of the role of law and their own relationship to the criminal law, there should be special courses to inform young people of the meaning of law and their responsibilities.

Once again this Geelong "Study for Action" cannot be regarded as a sufficient crime prevention planning exercise, but it will be seen that it is gradually taking shape. So far it has only been possible to deal with planning in a context of public participation, since this was the aspect that most interested the local people. Expertise was lacking both at Albury-Wodonga and Geelong—and can only be developed by better training in this field. Nevertheless, the interest is there, and it is being steadily developed with intercommunication between the areas concerned. The Institute's next investments in the process at Bathurst-Orange, Sydney, and Adelaide will further refine and concentrate the attention, developing expertise as it progresses. Alongside this, the Institute will be conducting courses for planners and criminal justice personnel to further improve the process and to provide the country with the techniques and data that it needs. Similarly, Albury-Wodonga and Geelong will continue to attract the interest and cooperation of the Institute in improving the approaches reported upon here.

There is still a long way to go before the planning of crime prevention becomes the professional service that it needs to be. But Australia has made a good start, and the degree of public participation is very encouraging.

Notes

1. *Planning a Low Crime Social Environment for Albury-Wodonga*, Australian Institute of Criminology, Canberra, 1976.

2. David Biles and Alex Copeland, *Crime in the Geelong Region*, Australian Institute of Criminology, 1976. This paper was specially compiled for the Geelong project, with the aid of the local police and the help of Dennis Challenger of the University of Melbourne.

Index

About the Author

William Clifford is Director of the Australian Institute of Criminology and has had wide experience in both economic and social planning and crime prevention. From 1968 to 1971 he was the United Nations Inter-regional Adviser on Social Planning which involved visiting and advising countries as widely dispersed as Iran, Venezuela, Togo, the Sudan and Laos.

Mr. Clifford was a member of the United Nations Evaluation Teams and served on a World Food Program Team of world experts which drew up a program for the future development of the Nile Delta in Egypt. He was also a member of a technical assistance programming mission to Kenya.

In crime prevention, Mr. Clifford pioneered criminological research in Africa and is the author of one of the first books on African criminology. He has also published a book on crime control in Japan where he served for some time as the United Nations Senior Adviser to the Asia and Far East Institute for the Prevention of Crime and the Treatment of Offenders.

Before moving to Australia Mr. Clifford was Director of the United Nations Crime Prevention and Criminal Justice Programs.